# I DANCED

Dear Mary,
Thank you for all
the care you have
given me.
Love
Dora Weber

# I DANCED

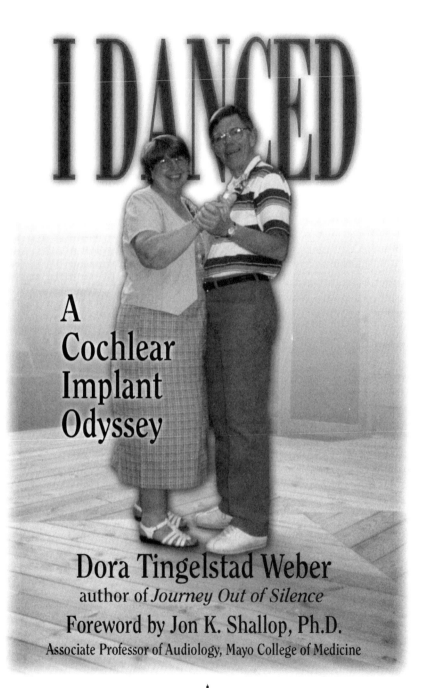

## A Cochlear Implant Odyssey

# Dora Tingelstad Weber
author of *Journey Out of Silence*

Foreword by Jon K. Shallop, Ph.D.
Associate Professor of Audiology, Mayo College of Medicine

Beaver's Pond Press, Inc.
Edina, Minnesota

"Bionic Humor and Joy" reprinted with permission of Mary Ann Schindler and Eleanor Tingelstad.

Weber Pedigree reprinted with permission of Dr. Richard Smith, Molecular Otolaryngology Research Laboratories, University of Iowa

Graphic and Photo of Spectra Nucleus 22 Implant reprinted with permission of Cochlear Americas

"My Grandchildren-My Motivation" reprinted with permission of *Cochlear Americas' Soundings* Summer 2000

"How It Works" reprinted with permission of Cochlear Americas

Graphic and Photo of Nucleus 3 System reprinted with permission of Cochlear Americas

"About Dora Weber" reprinted with permission of Likly Communications, Wilton, Conn.

Resetting the Speech Processor User Manual-Nucleus 24 Cochlear Implant System reprinted with permission of Cochlear Americas

Adjusting the Listening Controls User Manual-Nucleus 24 Cochlear Implant System reprinted with permission of Cochlear Americas

"Second cochlear implant gives gift of sound to Spring Lake Park resident" reprinted with permission of Jeff Coolman, Vice President and General Manager, Minnesota Sun Publications

"Hearing for the first time in a decade inspires woman to share her story" reprinted with permission of John Prinzler, *Houston County News,* LaCrescent, Minnesota, March 29, 2001

Photos - Dora's Nucleus 24 Contour ESPrit 3G; Dora's "Twins"; Dora's Smile reprinted with permission of Jon K. Shallop, Ph.D.

"Cochlear Implant Integrity Test" reprinted with permission of Jon K. Shallop, Ph.D. First printed in *Cochlear Implant News and Views.*

"Bilateral Cochlear Implants: Objective Assessment of Device Function and Variable Mode Programming in a case of Severe Facial Nerve Stimulation" reprinted with permission of Jon K. Shallop, Ph.D. and Colin L.W. Driscoll, M.D.

ISBN 1-59298-087-2

Library of Congress Catalog Number: 2004097557

Printed in the United States of America

08 07 06 05 04    6 5 4 3 2 1

Beaver's Pond Press, Inc.

7104 Ohms Lane, Suite 216
Edina, MN 55439
(952) 829-8818
www.beaverspondpress.com

to order, visit www.BookHouseFulfillment.com or call
1-800-901-3480. Reseller discounts available.

*Dedicated to Colin L.W. Driscoll, M.D.*
*and Jon K. Shallop, Ph.D.*
*for their encouragement which kept me dancing*

*With love and joy to*
*Jeffery, Justin, Jacob, Chelsea, Brandon and Ashley*
*and all future grandchildren*

## *Other Published Works by Dora Weber*

*Journey Out of Silence*
Published by Beaver's Pond Press, Inc., 1998

"Trees"
Published in *Best Poems of 1996*
by the National Library of Poetry

"Lumberjack's Music Brought Pair Together" (essay)
Published in *We Made Our Own Fun*
by Reminisce Books, 1995

"Yesterday's Tomorrow"
Published in *Poetic Voices of America, Spring 1993*
Sparrow Grass Poetry, Forum, Inc.

"Town of Heaven—State of Hope"
Published in *Distinguished Poets of America*
by the National Library of Poetry, 1993

"It's Spring—The Meadow's Reborn"
Published in *A Question of Balance*
by the National Library of Poetry, 1992

# Contents

# Acknowledgments

I wish to thank:

—my editor, Kathy Paulson, for the time and expertise she has provided in editing this book. I can say, without a doubt, that she is no longer a novice about the workings of the cochlear implant.

—my publisher, Milton Adams, for again believing in me and willingly taking on the unseen tasks that go along with publishing a book.

—Dr. Jon K. Shallop, Dr. Colin L.W. Driscoll, Sharon DeRosa, Dr. Saumi N. Merchant, Dr. Richard Smith, Pastor Paul Strawn, Aaron Parkinson, M.A., Terry D. Portis, Ed.D, Christine Writer, M.A., CCC-A and Sara Harms, Vice President of Consumer Marketing, Cochlear Americas for their submissions.

—Dr. Jon K. Shallop, Pastor Paul Strawn, Christine Writer, M.A., CCC-A, for reading the manuscript and for their valuable advice.

—my son, Scott M. Weber, for the beautiful design cover of the book.

—Mori Studio for all the help and assistance that went into creating a book I can proudly declare as "my book."

There are two very important persons, my husband, Myron, and my Lord and Savior, Jesus Christ, in my life. I thank Myron for the patience and support he has given me for 43 years. I thank my Lord and Savior, Jesus Christ, for charting a safe and successful course for me.

.

# Foreword

*by Jon K. Shallop, Ph.D.*

I am pleased to have this opportunity to write the foreword for this book. I have worked with cochlear implant patients now for over 20 years, both in the areas of clinical services and research. As I think back over my career, I recall many patients with wonderful stories about their successful use of a cochlear implant. Each patient has a special story, and they all point to the fact that cochlear implants have a profound effect on a person's life. With changing selection criteria, many more patients are now eligible to receive a cochlear implant than was the case 20 years ago. This includes young children down to the age of one, as well as some adults who have some residual hearing. The future of bilateral cochlear implants is a new area that is being explored, and one day we will all see the development of a completely implantable cochlear implant device.

I started my career in chemistry and physics. I was uncertain as to whether I wanted to be a high school teacher or a chemical engineer and work in my father's business. Somehow I got diverted from these ideas, and eventually worked my way into audiology. My first opportunity to work with cochlear implants was when I was an audiologist at Indiana University Medical Center. I vividly remember the day when Dr. Richard Miyamoto told me that we were going to start doing single channel cochlear implants. I told him I did not think it was a good idea, and that cochlear implants would probably not be very successful. How wrong I was!

Over the last 20 years, I have seen remarkable developments in cochlear implants, especially with the development of multichannel implants. We now have three choices for all of our patients; without a doubt, we are seeing good outcome results with all three of the FDA approved devices.

Dora Weber's case is very unique in that she now has two cochlear implants. Part of the decision for her to have a second implant was based on difficulties that she was having with her first implant. I first met Dora when I heard her give a talk at a National CIAI Convention in Minneapolis. I was impressed by her ability to articulate what she had been through and what she was now going through at that time. Through various channels, Dora ended up at Mayo Clinic where we were challenged to help her regain the use of her Nucleus 22 device. Some complications developed, and we had experience in dealing with some of those issues. It was very gratifying to our cochlear implant team that we were able to resolve some of the facial stimulation and other interference problems that had occurred with Dora's Nucleus 22 device. At present, she is able to use both of her devices on a daily basis, and our objective testing of both devices shows that she gets significant benefit from each device and the combination of the two devices provides her the most improvement in her listening skills.

I hope that this book will provide inspiration to others who are seeking a cochlear implant or other patients who now have a cochlear implant who just want to read about others in the same situation.

Sincerely,

Jon K. Shallop, Ph.D., CCC-A/SLP, F-AAA, F-ASHA
Consultant and Associate Professor
Mayo Clinic and Mayo College of Medicine
Rochester, Minnesota

# Introduction

When the processor switch of my Nucleus 22 cochlear implant was activated, I heard the voice of my husband, Myron, as I remembered it.

I believed I had reached the end of my journey out of silence. When my book, *Journey Out of Silence,* was published in 1998, I thought my travels were over. I had only been granted a respite before traveling on.

When I look back on the road I traveled after receiving my cochlear implant, I see a road that was easily traversed. I traveled on, stopping only for maintenance or to replace a worn part.

I don't recall when I got off that road and onto another. Changes with my hearing began to happen so gradually. One day I was coasting and the next, I was speeding down a road few had traveled. It was an exciting part of my journey. Six months later, I reached what I thought was my destination. Although the road then was a bit rough, I was content to remain where I was. Again, I was granted a respite before traveling on.

Where I was headed this time, I did not know. It was a frightening, uphill ride along a narrow road leading to a dead end. I grew weary and came close to ending my journey. Instead, I changed direction and traveled on until I reached familiar ground—a place where my journey had taken me once before.

There are several reasons why I wrote *I Danced,* continuing the story of the wonders of the cochlear implant. I want to share my experiences with sequential bilateral implants. My most important goal is to inspire others to try one more time—to go that extra mile.

One day, while waiting to have my Nucleus 24 Contour cochlear implant activated, I was watching *The View,* ABC's daytime morning chatfest. Country music singer, Lee Ann Womack, was a guest that day. I read along with closed captioning as she sang her hit song, "I Hope You Dance." The words of the song inspired me.

Throughout my life, the door to my hearing slowly closed. In 1986, it shut tight. Ten years later, after learning about the cochlear implant, I was faced with the choice of sitting it out or dancing. I chose to dance.

Four years later, when my hearing with my Nucleus 22 cochlear implant began to fade, I was given the chance to be sequentially implanted with a Nucleus 24 Contour cochlear implant. Again, I danced. In October, 2003, I was given the choice once more when my Nucleus 22 cochlear implant needed to be repositioned. Again, I chose to dance and I will continue to dance as many times as needed to retain the wonderful hearing I am experiencing with my sequential Nucleus cochlear implants. It is my wish that you, or someone you love, will not "sit it out," but will dance along with me.

*"Never give up. This may be your moment for a miracle."*
*—Greg Anderson*

"I still find each day too short for
all the thoughts I want to think,
all the walks I want to take,
all the books I want to read,
and all the friends I want to see."
—John Burroughs


AND ALL THE THINGS I WANT TO HEAR
—Dora Weber

# Part One

## Stop Over
## 1996-2000

M any wonderful things happened during the four years after I received my Nucleus 22 Cochlear Implant. Every day was a new day and the feeling of awe I felt on the first day of my activation never left me. My cochlear implant made a world of difference in my life and in the lives of those I love.

# Enduring Love

*"And then, at long last, I was placed in the loving arms of Myron, the guy I would spend the rest of my life with . . ."*
—from *Journey Out of Silence*

I had just turned 22 the August before I met Myron. I had several boyfriends after I graduated but I was not dating anyone at that time. One after another, my roommates, friends and classmates, were meeting the men of their dreams and getting engaged or married.

Here I was, 22 years old—an old maid by the standards of the 50's—and I didn't have any prospective courters. I was in dire straits, indeed.

I didn't have any girlfriends to go with me to look for one. Actually, I didn't even have to leave my apartment to go looking for him. He came to find me!

My roommates and I bought an old black and white TV that often went on the blink and we were going broke paying repairmen to fix it. My roommate's boyfriend had a perfect solution. He brought his roommate and handyman, Myron, over to fix it. As payment, we invited him to stay for dinner. He asked me to go bowling with him the following evening. After a four-month courtship, we married and he packed his bags and joined me on my journey out of silence.

It was not my practice when dating to inform the guys of my hearing loss until we had gone on several dates. With Myron, it was different. He knew before he met me. He also knew, before our wedding, that I was still paying for my second stapes mobilization as well as making payments on the binaural hear-

*The Weber family celebrating Christmas in 2003*

ing aids I had recently purchased. I do think he was surprised, a year later, when my hearing went down after the birth of our first son.

I don't believe he expected that our journey would take me through the many surgeries it did. He took our wedding vow, in good times and in bad, seriously. He rejoiced with me at my successful stapedectomy and he comforted me when two were unsuccessful. When my hearing, along with my disposition, declined and I began to make life miserable for him, he stuck by me. I am sure that during those times he didn't find traveling with me much fun.

Just to get through the day made me tired and by the time Myron got home from work, I was testy and unreasonable. I didn't even try to understand what he said to me. More often than not, what I thought he said was not what he said and I would imagine that he was "putting me down." I would hurry to our bedroom, slam the door and lie on our bed and cry. The first few times this happened, he followed and tried to console me. Even if I had been able to understand him, I would not have listened. I was feeling sorry for myself. After going through this routine a few times, he learned to leave me alone.

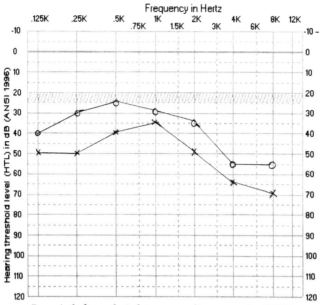

*Dora's left and right ear audiograms in 1957
prior to stapesmobilization surgeries*

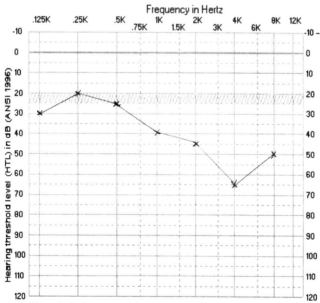

*Dora's left ear audiogram following her 1957
stapesmobilization surgery*

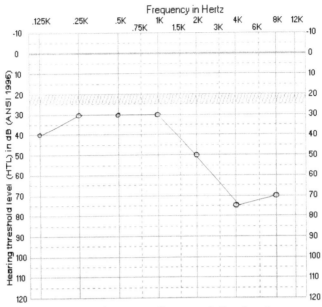

*Dora's right ear audiogram following her*
*1959 stapesmobilization surgery*

I remember one episode. I call it that because it was not an argument. An argument is a contest in reasoning and I surely was not being reasonable. It was particularly bad. I didn't just go into our room and cry.

I took my rings off. We didn't speak for days.

Then, one day, Myron came home from work and told me that, while listening to the radio on the way to work that morning, he heard about a marriage counselor who counseled over the telephone. He had called her.

My first thought was, *How dare he do that without consulting me!* Then, I got really worried. Our marriage was not a game to him. He was taking it seriously and he thought we needed help.

I was afraid to find out what he had been told. Did she tell him to leave? I finally gained the courage to ask him. He had been told that we should do more things together. That would have been good advice for the average couple but not for us. It would have given me more opportunities when I would not hear him and the resentment would have built up even more.

This was our last major disagreement. Soon after, I underwent an unsuccessful revisal stapedectomy and became profoundly deaf in both ears. Somehow, when that happened, it was a relief. I no longer had to struggle to hear with my hearing aid as turning up the volume did not enable me to hear better. It only caused the terrible feedback (squealing) that I could not hear but which was clearly audible to others. Continuously, I was told to "Turn your hearing aid down." When I decided to stop wearing my hearing aid, the stress caused by my struggle to hear was greatly alleviated.

Much to the delight of Myron, I became easier to get along with and we began communicating by writing notes. Ten years later, at the activation of my cochlear implant, I heard his voice

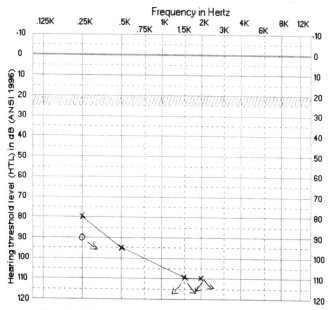

*Dora's left and right ear audiograms in 1985*
*after unsuccessful revisal stapedectomy surgery*

as I remembered it to be. We have not had to resort to writing notes since.

My cochlear implant brought so many wonderful changes to our marriage. Myron became much happier and more relaxed. He was very happy when I was able to use the telephone again.

I think he was more thrilled than I was the first time I called him at work. I don't remember the reason for the call but that doesn't matter. We weren't far into the conversation before he said, "This is so nice!" We spent the next few minutes laughing and hugging across the telephone lines. After spending much of his workday on the telephone, he was ready to let me take my own calls and make my own appointments. He wasn't sorry, either, that he no longer had to tag after me to those appointments. This was beneficial to me as well. The doctor and dentist could no longer speak to me through him. They had to do business with me.

We did not need a marriage counselor to tell us to spend more time together. It came naturally. Myron had been attending a home Bible study for several years before my hearing was restored. I joined him the first Monday evening after my cochlear implant was activated. We frequently went out to dinner, to Minnesota Timberwolves' basketball games, to concerts and to movies.

The first movie we went to was *Titanic*. The sound was great and I was able to follow the conversations easily. I was especially thrilled to be able to hear a humorous conversation between Jack and Rose. The ship was breaking up. Jack was chained to a pole down in the galley; the water was rising rapidly. After several minutes of frantically searching for him, Rose found him and tried unsuccessfully to free him. Finally, she gave up and went in search for a tool she could use.

As she left, Jack shouted after her, his humor intact, "I'll wait right here!"

To be able to hear that and laugh along with the audience was a highlight. It did get pretty noisy towards the end of the movie. I wanted to decrease the microphone sensitivity but it was so dark in the theatre, I wasn't able to find the correct setting. I vowed to take a flashlight with me to our next movie.

When I think back on the times I would want to take a drive up to northern Minnesota to visit family, I remember the hassle I had to go through to get Myron to go. By the time he consented, I was so worn out and frustrated that it took all the enjoyment out of going.

Perhaps the reason for his unwillingness to travel with me was because I could not hear him. He had only the radio for company while I slept or read a book. It must have been quite lonely for him. After I received my implant, we took many mini-trips in Minnesota, Wisconsin and Iowa. We either talked nonstop or listened to the radio or our CDs.

But the change that I think made Myron the happiest was that he could now argue with me. One day while we were in the middle of a disagreement, he began to laugh. I certainly did not think it was funny but I didn't get up and run into our bedroom.

"What's so funny?" I demanded.

Laughing even more, he answered, "It's just so much fun to argue with you now!"

There were several times after that when I sensed that he got me started on purpose so I thought I would make it even more fun for him. Sometimes I let him win!

# My Reasons for Hearing

**M**y relationships with my four sons were much more courteous than that with Myron. When I questioned them about what it was like growing up with a hearing-impaired mom, they acted surprised that I had asked. They assured me they had not found anything amiss. By the time I began to have a difficult time with my loss, Chuck and Ken were out on their own and Dave and Scott were kept busy with school activities, work and sports. They weren't home to witness my dramatics.

By the time Chuck, Ken and Dave had married, I was more accepting of my deafness and much more relaxed. If I could not understand their wives, Sharon, Janine, and Allison, they communicated the way Myron and the boys did—they wrote notes. It was more difficult to do so at our family gatherings as then the conversation flowed at a faster pace.

I missed a lot of good chatting but I didn't get up and run away. Just to have something to do, I would get up and start clearing the dishes. I did receive some looks of displeasure and I can understand why. It must have been quite annoying when they were trying to visit. Washing dishes is not a quiet task.

Myron and I had to wait a few years before our first grandchildren were born. I was satisfied with my adopted lifestyle until Jeffery and Jacob began to talk. It would be a long time before they could write me notes and I could not wait that long. I wanted to hear their voices then.

I began taking care of Jeffery when he was eight weeks old. The year that he was three, he gave me a beautiful framed poem for Christmas.

It hangs in our bathroom and I read it often.

## Walking with Grandma

I like to walk with Grandma
Her steps are short like mine
She doesn't say, "Now hurry up"
She always takes her time.

I like to walk with Grandma
Her eyes see things like mine do . . .
Wee pebbles bright, a funny cloud,
Half hidden drops of dew.

Most people have to hurry
They don't stop to see . . .
I'm glad that God made Grandma
Unrushed and young like me.
                    —*Author Unknown*

When I began to write this book, I discovered the true meaning of the words. It speaks of a grandma and her grandchild seeing things in the same way—not of hearing them.

Jeffery and I spent countless hours outdoors when I took care of him. We went for many walks, often stopping at the park to play. We were never in a hurry to arrive as there was so much to see and "hear" along the way.

We paused to watch the robin, with its head cocked, listening for an unsuspecting worm to bring home to her babies. We picked dandelion bouquets for Jeffery's mom and when the blooms turned to seeds, we watched as the wind whipped up the little airplanes and sent them flying through the air. We stopped to observe the busy ants building their villages and the bees as they flew from flower to flower gathering nectar to take back to their honey factories.

I did not need my hearing to enjoy those things. I used my eyes but some things were created to be heard. For those, I drew from my memory bank and heard them through Jeffery's little ears.

We heard the snap of a twig as he broke it, the crackling of rocks and the squishing of sand as we walked across the parking lot. We listened to the screeching of the chains as I pushed him in the swing and the swoosh as he slid down the slide. We heard the clap of the thunder and the pelting of rain against the windows during a summer thunderstorm, the crunch of leaves under our feet in the fall and the snow in winter. In the spring, we enjoyed the tinkling of the melting snow as it rushed down the street and into the sewer.

I "heard" all those sounds and they were wonderful but the sounds I most wanted to hear, the voices of my grandsons, Jeffery and Jacob, remained silent to me. They had not been stored in my memory. They were my inspiration to continue with my journey out of silence and they became my reasons for hearing.

After I received my cochlear implant, I heard Jeffery say, "Let's go play, Grandma." With tears streaming down my face, I listened as Jacob sang, "Home on the Range." I will never know if I heard them as Grandpa did but they sounded fine to me and I understood every word.

Jeffery was the easiest to understand as he was the older and had not yet broken his habit of looking at me when he spoke as he had been told to do.

It was so much fun to watch my grandsons grow. In no time, they were in kindergarten and I was attending their spring musicals, reading to their classes and attending Bible quizzes and spelling bees. They became involved in sports at such an early age, it was almost as if they went from wearing their soft little baby shoes right into their sport shoes.

In the fall and winter, it was soccer for Jeffery and hockey for Jacob. In the spring and summer, their fancy turned to baseball. They both began with T-ball. The little batters would hit the ball off a tee. After two summers, they graduated to coach pitch. Their coach pitched to them while a player covered the pitching spot, chasing any balls that were hit or trying to catch a fly ball. Everyone on the team had a chance to play that covetous position and Grandpa and I were at the game when it was Jacob's turn. He made us proud!

The coach pitched the ball and wham! The batter hit it and it headed straight for Jacob. He held out his arm and the baseball landed with a thump right in his glove. The look of surprise that came to his face should have been captured on camera.

Then reality hit. The fans cheered and a smile took the place of his surprise. He jumped up and down while the fans cheered. The following day, when we went to Jeffery's game, I told him that Jacob had caught a fly.

Jeffery looked at me, a puzzled look on his face and asked, "What did he do with it?"

I had neglected to say "fly ball" and the poor little guy was wondering where Jacob had kept his "fly" until he could get home to put it in a jar.

Jacob's little sister and our first granddaughter, Chelsea, was born in July, just two months before I received my cochlear implant. She was the first grandchild I heard cry. After having been surrounded by four sons and two grandsons for so many years, it took me some time to learn the ways of a little girl. It also took Chelsea some time to get over her shyness with me but once she did, she was a fun loving little girl who loved to laugh and she liked to make me laugh as well.

She had been in gymnastics almost as long as she had been walking and was a natural. Whenever Grandpa and I went over to baby-sit Chelsea and her brother, Jacob, she would take out her CD player, put her CD in and entertain us with a private performance.

She was flawless and serious almost to the end of her routine. Then, I saw the mischief building in her eyes and I knew we were in for a surprise ending. Instead of ending her routine with a handspring, followed by the splits, she ended it with a plop—right on her fanny.

Chelsea would lie there, her face covered, and laugh. Every so often she would peek up at me to see if I was laughing, too. After having done this a few times, I knew it was intentional and that we had to wait until her recital to see just how well she performed. Even then, she wore her impish grin but we were proud of her. She went through her routine without a hitch.

Every year, for the next three years, I was given one more reason to hear. Jeffery's little brother, Justin, was born the following spring. Unlike Jeffery, Jacob, and Chelsea, who were sleeping when I visited them shortly after their births, Justin was wide awake and crying lustily.

It had been so long since I had heard a newborn baby cry. When the nurse placed him in my arms, I just sat rocking him and listening to him cry. I heard some sounds I had never heard before—the cracking and squeaking of his little body and I was amazed and a little bit frightened. I was able to hear his lusty cries as they changed into the merriest giggles I have ever heard.

I think Justin was born to make others laugh and he soon became my ally. If no one else laughed at my jokes, I could count on him. His laugh was so contagious that I had to be very careful not to make him laugh in church. I did not want to distract the congregation or worse yet, cause them to become infected.

Our youngest grandchildren, Brandon and his little sister Ashley, both blue-eyed blondes, were born a year apart. Brandon was born Jan. 2,1998, his grandpa's birthday, and Ashley arrived a year later. I heard their soft little voices but was not quite able, without their mom as interpreter, to understand much more than simple phrases that they repeated over and over.

"You do, Grandma." "Do it again, Grandma." "Play with me, Grandma." "Read it again, Grandma."

Grandpa and I baby-sat with them for a week after they moved into their new house. I lost track, after the first four times, just how many times I read, *Wheels on the Bus* to Ashley. I didn't need an interpreter to understand, "Read it one more time, Grandma."

One morning, Brandon and Ashley went down to the basement to ride their little cars. I was up in the kitchen fixing lunch.

*Dora's reasons for hearing—her six wonderful grandchildren, Jeffery, Brandon, Chelsea (holding Snickers), Justin, Jacob, and Ashley*

All of a sudden, I heard, "Grandma, Grandma, come down here. Ashley wiped out!"

I stopped what I was doing and hurried down the stairs. Ashley had indeed wiped out but it had been staged! She was lying under her car, her leg pinned under the tire. I moved the car, picked her up, laid her on the couch and pretended to give her first aid. That was the beginning of another fun game. It was so nice to be able to hear and understand them.

Several years ago, our grandsons, Jeffery and Jacob, began a tradition of ending our family gatherings in grand style. They spent all afternoon rehearsing the script for a puppet show they would perform at the close of the day. They set up chairs in a row, sold "tickets" and even had a drawing for a door prize.

As much as they rehearsed the script, most of the dialogue was ad lib. I ate up every word. If I did not hear what they said, I had someone repeat it. I had sat through too many silent performances. There was not a more enthusiastic fan than Grandma. I was very proud of my "reasons for hearing."

# Friends, Birds, Crickets and Frogs

I feel so blessed to have had such wonderful support from my friends and neighbors while I was hearing impaired and after I became deaf. When I speak to prospective cochlear implant candidates, I hear the same story over and over. When they became deaf, their friends could not cope with their deafness and they were abandoned.

During those years, there were many times I wanted to stay home when I was invited out to lunch. It would have been so much easier for all of us but my friends insisted that I go along and, most times, I was glad they did.

They always went out of their way to help me place my order, sometimes talking over the other. After my hearing was restored, just out of habit, they remained ever watchful and if I was having problems placing my order, they stepped in.

I always carried a notepad and pen with me which we used for communicating. We went through so much paper that, following my cochlear implant, my friend Barb was prompted to comment that the paper companies would soon be going out of business.

Barb, my backdoor neighbor and friend, is the one I visit with the most. We have much in common. We both have four sons, belong to the same church and we share a love for the outdoors, spending many summer hours outside.

We have adjacent backyard flower gardens. It is not often that one of us is out working alone. If one of us looks out the window and sees the other, we drop whatever we are doing and go out to

*Dora and her backdoor friends of 32 years: Barb, Colleen, JoAnn, and Pat, celebrating Barb's birthday.*

*Dora and Barb spend many summer hours together in their adjacent flower gardens.*

be together. We don't get any weeding done—that waits until the other is gone for the day. We just enjoy our flowers.

Barb teaches me the names of flowers that are unfamiliar to me and together we enjoy the birds. Before my hearing was restored, she listened to their songs while I watched them flit from bird feeder to tree to birdbath. I was familiar with those who frequented our backyard so she didn't have to teach me their names; after I was able to hear, she began to teach me their songs.

Poor Barb. I think I nearly drove her crazy that first spring. Whenever I heard a bird sing, I asked her, "What bird is that? What bird is that?"

She thought it was quite fun at first but after I asked her what the cardinal's song was for the millionth time, I think she became a bit irritated. Even though it was hard for me to do, I let up for a while and began to be more watchful.

One day, I just could not let a song go by without finding out what bird was doing all that chirping. It was late afternoon and we were sitting by my picnic table. I kept hearing this beautiful chirping. I looked in the trees, up at the telephone lines and along the fence.

There was not a bird in sight. The chirping continued without a pause. Since I had not heard that bird before, I thought it would be okay to ask Barb about it even though she showed no signs of even hearing it.

"Barb," I said, "please tell me what bird is singing."

She gave me a puzzled look and said, "I don't hear a bird."

I knew I was hearing very well with my implant. I knew, too, that there was nothing wrong with Barb's hearing. I told her to listen. She cocked her head, a smile came over her face and she started to laugh.

"Dora, the bird that you are hearing," Barb explained, "is a cricket over in the flowers by the foundation of your house!"

When I later told Myron, he laughed, too, and said, "It doesn't sound like a bird to me."

I couldn't get enough of listening to the birds. Springbrook Nature Center is not far from our home. In the 25 years we had lived there, we had never taken advantage of that center. I am sure the reason was that it was not fun to go somewhere when I couldn't hear but now I was drawn to it.

One Saturday morning, Myron and I got up early before it was too hot and we drove over there. We parked the car and started walking along a trail. It was such a beautiful, tranquil place yet it was alive with the wonders of nature.

Wildflowers bloomed everywhere and berries hung from vines. Turtles crawled up the muddy banks, slid back down and tried again. Baby ducklings tumbled over one another in their haste to follow their mother down to the water. Beavers were hard at work building their dams and ducks glided in and sat watching them work. There was everything there except the birds we had come to hear.

The scenery changed as we walked. While strolling through the dense woodland, I thought of the stories Mama had told me about living in the wilderness of northern Minnesota. She could hear the howling of the wolves when she walked to school. I half expected one to jump out at us.

As we came out of the woods onto the prairie land, it reminded me of the *Little House on the Prairie* books and I looked around to see if the Ingalls' children were running through the tall grass. All I saw as we came around a bend in the trail was a swinging bridge in the distance which was suspended over a pond of water. I began to hear a strange sound as we came closer.

I thought, *Aha! I'm hearing some different birds after all!*

The sound became louder, then grew softer and softer until it faded away. It started up again, quietly at first and building to a loud crescendo before fading away. Over and over it happened.

When we reached the bridge, I paused to listen. Then, I knew it was not the birds. There was a city street just beyond a grove of trees and I thought it might be traffic but I soon ruled that out. There was not a car in sight when I heard the noise. I just could not leave without finding out what was making that sound.

I asked Myron, "What is that sound?"

Nonchalantly, he replied, "Oh, there are a lot of frogs over on the shore."

I froze. I could not remember the last time I had heard the croaking of a frog and now I was hearing perhaps hundreds of them. Tears began to roll down my cheeks unchecked. The only thing I had to wipe them with was my hand so I must have looked a mess to passing strollers. I didn't care. I'm sure they wondered why I was crying. I'm sure, too, that had they known, they would have been surprised that the croaking of the frogs could make a grown woman cry. I did not want to leave. It was only with a promise that we would return that I followed Myron off the bridge.

Our last trek of the day was through meadowland. As we walked, I thought of the many bouquets of wildflowers I had picked to bring home to Mama and I recalled a poem I had written.

### It's Spring—The Meadow's Reborn

It's Spring—The meadow awakens to the warmth
of the golden sun. The snow that had
once been its blanket has melted and
now it is gone.

It's Spring—The clover leaf pushes its fragile head
up through the ground. With their leaflets,
the meadow, they'll dress; pink flowers
adorning the gown.

23

It's Spring—Wild flowers are blooming. Perfume gently
floats through the air. With beauty, the
meadow, they're grooming their garlands
festooning its hair.

It's Spring—The meadow is reborn with all things so
freshly renewed. The faded brown dress
that she had worn is replaced with a green,
yellow, blue.

It's Spring—The Meadow's reborn!

I thought, *How alike is the rebirth of a meadow in spring to
the rebirth of my hearing.*

# Strangers

*"One of the advantages of being deaf is that the loss of one sense sharpens all your others and gives you the perceptions that many hearing people may not have. The only difficult thing is that so many people think there is something the matter with your mind because it takes you a little while to get accustomed to the way they talk; to be looked upon as a moron when you are extra bright and extra disciplined must take a lot of patience."*

—Eleanor Roosevelt

Long ago, when I was a hearing-impaired teenager, I went out of my way to avoid strangers. It was not because I was afraid physical harm might come to me; it was the mental anguish that, unknowingly, they could cause me. I did not want anyone to think I was dumb, a stigma that was associated with deafness at the time.

I began bluffing. It was easy to cover up my loss to my family or friends but not with a stranger. Then, I was given two choices. I could let them think I was shy, which I certainly wasn't, or I could appear to be not-so-bright, which also was not true. It was my natural love for people that caused me to appear to be not-so-bright.

Whenever I was caught with strangers and I could not hear what they were saying, I would pretend I did and I would get away with a sweet smile. Not so, when I was asked a question and did not understand. Oh, my, those were embarrassing times. I could feel the blood rush to my face. If I did not understand on the second try, knowing that I would know the answer to a simple question about my age or grade, I would say, "I don't know" and walk away.

For a time after an encounter, I would wonder if I would experience any repercussions from these one-sided conversations. Perhaps someone I knew would hear about it and make me feel like a fool. I was continuously thinking of ways to cover up, not only situations such as this, but my hearing loss as well. Nothing much ever came of my worries; life went on but I was always on my guard. The feeling of inadequacy that these encounters gave me followed me into my adult life.

In 1986, shortly after I underwent an unsuccessful revisal stapedectomy in my right ear, I became profoundly deaf in both ears. The tinnitus that I had coped with all my life became almost intolerable. It rang. It buzzed. It roared and it hissed. Day after day, I listened to what sounded like the voice of an announcer on a badly tuned radio station.

One day, when the tinnitus was particularly bad, I went for a walk. I walked and walked and soon I forgot about the noise in my head. Walking became my therapy and sometimes I walked as often as three times a day.

When I walked, I was often asked directions to here and there. I don't know the reason except perhaps it was that I was outside so much and became a target for inquiries or it could have been God's plan. Perhaps He wanted to keep me in the world.

It became an everyday occurrence for a car to pull up along side me, the window rolled down, and the driver would ask, "Can you tell me where . . . ?" I never got farther than that so again, I had two choices—either appear unfriendly and walk on by or bluff. I had lived in the neighborhood for close to 25 years and I knew every street so, quite likely, I would have been able to help but I was never able to understand where it was they wanted to go.

Once again, my love for people won out and I bluffed my way through. I pretended I was new in the neighborhood. This bothered me very much as I love to help people and I knew I would have been able to help had I only been able to hear.

After I had my cochlear implant, the tinnitus in my right ear disappeared and the hearing I received with my implant successfully masked it in my left ear. I no longer needed to take my walks for therapy. By then, it had become a habit so I continued walking every day. Guess what! Everyone drove right past me. They all knew how to get to where they were going. I had to wait for several months before someone got lost and needed my help.

Early one Saturday morning, I was about to turn onto the street leading to the McDonald's Restaurant where I stopped for coffee. A car carrying several teenagers slowed down and came to a stop by me. The window rolled down and a young man asked, "Do you know where the Emmanuel Christian Center is?"

Wow, I had heard him on the first try and I knew the answer, too! I felt like I was about to answer the million dollar question on the "Who Wants to Be a Millionaire?" show. A smile lit up my face as I walked to the car and gave them directions.

"Go down 81st St. until you come to Terrace Rd. Take a left on Terrace and go to Osborne Rd. Take a right on Osborne and go about a block and you will see it on your right. It is a huge church so you won't miss it."

I will never forget that day. Maybe—just maybe—they told their friends about the friendly lady who was so happy to help them.

After that, I knew I no longer needed to avoid strangers and I began to bond with everyone. If a package was delivered to the house, I chatted with the delivery person. If a repairman came, I no longer went into another room and pretended I was busy. If I met another walker on my walks, I didn't look away. I smiled and said, "Good morning," and sometimes stopped for a chat. I bonded with our county assessor when he came to see if we had made any improvements on our house. I even listened as door to door salesmen and those running for government offices during election time gave me their sales pitches. And when I was at the mall—ah! That is a story in itself.

One of the reasons we moved to our area was because I do not drive and churches, schools, a hospital, dental and medical clinics were near enough for me to walk. I often do my shopping at a big mall which is also within walking distance.

One morning, I arrived early before the stores opened so I sat down in a chair across from Montgomery Ward to wait. I noticed a nicely dressed man, who looked to be about my age, sitting across from me.

He smiled and said, "Good morning." Of course, I couldn't ignore him so I answered, "Good morning."

I don't remember who initiated the conversation that followed. Soon, he moved over to a chair closer to me and began telling me his life story. He was a widower with grown children. When he whipped out his billfold and began showing me photos of his grandchildren, I began to feel uneasy.

I was about to go into the gift shop that had just opened when the doors of Montgomery Ward slid open. I got up and went in. He was right behind me. Then, I didn't think anything of it but whenever I looked up from the merchandise I was looking at, there he was! I walked to the entrance leading to the mall and he came too.

"I have to go," I said.

I hurried down the hallway of the mall and didn't look back until I was at the mall exit. I glanced quickly over my shoulder. He was nowhere in sight. Scurrying across the parking lot, I made it in record time. As I crossed the street, I noticed a nearby garage sale and decided to stop there to catch my breath.

As I walked up the driveway to the sale, I spotted another man, this one perhaps a little older than I was, standing near the garage entrance. He greeted me so, of course, I smiled and returned the greeting.

I went into the garage and began rummaging through the merchandise that was spread out on the tables. Out of the corner of my eye, I could see someone standing by me but I assumed it was another customer. Gradually, I realized that wherever I moved, this person followed me. I was afraid to look up. I thought I would see the fellow from the mall.

Nope, it was another fellow—the man who greeted me at the door. I threw down what I had intended to purchase and made a beeline to the door. I didn't stop to look back until I was a block down the street. When I did pause, I saw him standing at the bottom of the driveway.

Maybe he had tried to follow me but I had been too fast for him. I kept walking as fast as I could until I was home. My son, Dave, was washing his car in our driveway but I didn't stop to talk. I hurried into the house.

After I had calmed down, I began to think about the events of the morning. *Could it be possible,* I wondered, *that these fellows were trying to pick me up?* I decided to ask Dave what he thought. A smile came to his face as I talked.

When I had finished. he laughed and said, "Sure, Mom, of course they were trying to pick you up! You are still attractive so be careful who you flirt with!"

Me, flirt? I was just having a friendly conversation. I had never learned how to flirt and I never gave anyone a chance to try to pick me up. I wouldn't talk to them. Now, here I was, a 60-year-old grandma and I was accused of flirting and being picked up. I began to feel a bit smug.

Did I change my ways? I have to admit that I didn't, as it is in my nature to be friendly. But I did do something different. I made sure everyone knew I was happily married. I certainly did not want to miss an opportunity to share the wonderful gift that had been given to me. Maybe he, or someone he loved, needed to hear about the cochlear implant!

# That All May Hear

On August 12, 1957, after a stapes mobilization, and on August 10, 1967, after a stapedectomy, I received wonderful birthday presents—improved hearing in my left ear. Possibly because I did have some hearing in my right ear, the improvement was not dramatic enough to inspire me to share it with others. Both times, my hearing was taken away from me and I became profoundly deaf in both ears at the age of 48.

Ten years later, again in August and four days before my 58th birthday, I received another present. My hearing was restored with my Nucleus 22 cochlear implant. This time, after having been deaf for 10 years, the impact of suddenly being able to hear again was so great and I was inspired to give back. I had been given so much that I knew, however much I gave back, it would never be enough.

In the hope that others might be helped, I wanted to share the wonderful gift I had been given. Since I like to write, what better way was there than to write my story and submit it to newspapers where so many could be reached. The natural place was my hometown of Pelican Rapids, Minnesota and the neighboring towns of Fergus Falls and Detroit Lakes.

I also embarked on a very amateurish speaking mission when I accepted an invitation to speak at a District 5M-6 Lions midwinter convention in St. Paul. For several days after I received the invitation, I was so excited, I was floating on air. Then, as convention time drew near, I became very nervous and regressed back to when I was a scared teenager waiting to give a social studies speech. I remember that time well.

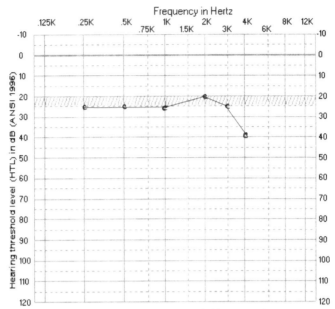

*Dora's right ear audiogram following the 1996*
*implantation of her Nucleus 22 cochlear implant system*

I was nervous about getting up in front of my classmates. What frightened me more, however, was that I would not be able to hear the questions they would ask me when I finished. Day after day went by while I sat and listened to the other speeches, trying to come up with a solution. I became more nervous with each passing day.

Then, I came up with a brilliant idea. With 15 minutes left of the class period, I raised my hand. I walked up to the podium and began to speak. I did not stop talking until the bell rang, signaling the end of the period. No time for questions. I walked back to my desk, gathered up my books and went on to my next class.

This time I didn't fret over my fears for long. I decided to confide in my audiologist. Her advice, "Speak from your heart and the words will flow," didn't sound too promising.

When I was introduced, I felt the blood rush to my face but

I took a deep breath and did as she advised. She was right. The words did flow freely. In fact, so freely that I encountered a different problem. How was I to staunch the flow? I had so much to share that I did not want to stop speaking. Eventually, I did stop and when I was questioned, I found out I didn't need a bell to save me. I heard the questions clearly, even those that came from the back of the room.

After that presentation, I received more requests to share my story, both in writing and speaking. I was invited to be the guest speaker at the spring meeting of the Trinity Lutheran Church ladies' group in Detroit Lakes, Minnesota and also to share my story in the District 5M-10 Lions Club newsletter. If anyone had told me prior to receiving my cochlear implant that I would be speaking and writing like this, I would not have listened. One day, I read this little poem that appeared after the article I had written and it all came into perspective.

## Isn't It Strange

Isn't it strange that princes and kings
And clowns that caper in sawdust rings
and common people like you and me
are builders of eternity?
Each is given a bag of tools
a shapeless mass, a book of rules
and each must make—ere life is flown
a stumbling block or a stepping stone.
—*Author Unknown*

It spoke to me. All through my life, one stumbling block after another had been placed in my path. That shapeless mass took form when my hearing was restored with my cochlear implant.

The tools I needed had been locked up in my heart and now they were free for me to use. The opportunities to use them came spontaneously. I took stumbling blocks and changed them into stepping stones.

Two months after my Nucleus 22 was activated, I began participating in the research of the cochlear implant. In an effort to help scientists find out how electrical hearing differs from acoustic hearing, I participated in many psychoacoustic and speech recognition experiments.

For four years, I participated in research twice weekly to listen to beeps and to differentiate between phonemes such as aba and ada, ana and ama and aka and ata. (A phoneme is a group of words taken to be the same identical sound but differing by the position and movement of the speaker's vocal cords—such as the first sound in the words pen, pin, pan, pun.)

Some of the experiments ran for several weeks so they did get quite tedious but the scientists were great to work with and the time flew by. Just to know that the information gathered on my performance could be used to help improve devices for future generations was enough to keep me returning week after week.

While working in the research lab, I learned about the National Institute on Deafness and Other Communication Disorders (NIDCD) National Temporal Bone Registry and was encouraged to have my temporal bones donated to research upon my death. Because of my genetic otosclerosis, this has always been of interest to me but I had never sought information. Now that I had the form with the address, I could not procrastinate. I filled it out and placed it in my mailbox.

I received a donor enrollment packet and an information brochure about temporal bone donations. I pledged my temporal bones and now Myron and I carry my signed pledge cards in our billfolds. The study will provide a better understanding of the benefits different people receive from the implant and what surgical strategies might be used during implantation.

Since I was at the research laboratory twice a week, I decided I would look into volunteering on the mornings of the days when I worked in research. After going through the orientation and completing the necessary requirements of a volunteer, I received my placement as a reader in a literacy program called Project Read.

My teenage dream was to become a teacher and it came somewhat true. My students were the little patients in the pediatric clinic who were waiting to see their doctors. The playroom of the clinic was my classroom, transformed into a magical place. The children sat on a magic carpet and were transported by their imaginations into another world. They were excited to hear a story and to receive a gift book of their very own to take home. The two hours I spent reading was a very enjoyable and rewarding experience. What I received from the children far outweighed what they received from me.

*Reading to the children in Project Read at the pediatric clinic is a "magic time."*

I had a large selection of books for the children to choose from but they had their favorites. The three I read over and over were *The Adventures of Franklin the Turtle, The Adventures of Corduroy,* a stuffed bear, and *Love You Forever,* a story depicting a mother's love for her son as he goes through the stages of childhood and becomes a man. All through her son's life, this mother would go into his room at night and if he was sleeping, she would pick him up, rock him and sing, "I'll love you forever, I'll like you for always, as long as I'm living, my baby you'll be."

Each time, when I came to that song, I asked the children to sing along with me. Although a few were shy, most were willing and by the last time, almost all were singing along—even the parents, many with tears in their eyes.

When my time spent reading to the children was over, there was an hour to fill before beginning my session in the research laboratory. Often, I spent the time in the waiting room of the cochlear implant center, talking to prospective candidates.

It didn't take me long to realize that, other than sharing the wonderful news that I could now hear, there was much about the implant of which I was not knowledgeable. I wanted to become better educated. I thought other recipients might feel the same way. I believed that organizing a Minnesota chapter of Cochlear Implant Association International (CIAI) would be an excellent way to reach everyone.

I expressed my thoughts to my audiologist. She was supportive of the idea and with her help, questionnaires were sent out to patients of the cochlear implant center and to other Minnesota residents who were patients at neighboring centers. I received a favorable response and an organizational meeting was held.

Four meetings were held yearly with guests speaking on various subjects of interest to the cochlear implant candidates and users. We learned about assistive listening devices (ALDs), the mapping process, aural-oral rehabilitation and why we needed to visit a psychologist as well as many other interesting subjects.

A newsletter with contributions from members was published four times a year. My contribution was a "Bionic Humor and Joy" column, a compilation of humorous and joyful experiences of my own as well as those of other members. One of the first ones I wrote was about some alarming sounds that my friend, Mary Ann, and my sister, Eleanor, heard.

### Bionic Humor and Joy
#### *Dora Weber*

The joy and humor that I derive from being able to hear again is as overwhelming today as it was the day I received my cochlear implant. Then, too, there are times when hearing sounds never before heard or those long forgotten can be quite alarming. My friend, Mary Ann, and my sister, Eleanor, can attest to that.

Mary Ann's story took place last summer when, on a clear, quiet evening, she and her husband were doing yard work on their farm. Mary Ann was busy weeding her flowers when all of a sudden, she heard an unfamiliar sound. She looked all around but couldn't see anything unusual.

She was puzzled but, instead of asking her husband what the sound was, she wanted to discover it for herself.

She stood up and turned this way and that. When she was facing the highway which was some distance away, an ambulance came speeding down the road. Then she knew what she had been hearing.

"Aha!" she cried, "I can hear an ambulance!"

Mary Ann heard it again when it returned to town.

The setting of my sister's story is the kitchen of her home in Pelican Rapids, Minnesota, shortly after she had received her cochlear implant. After placing an angel food cake in the oven, Eleanor was relaxing by reading the newspaper. Suddenly she jumped up.

The quiet evening, as well as her nerves, were shattered by a high pitched buzzing sound. Her first thought was that her processor had gone haywire. Then she looked out the window and spied a beatup truck going by and she thought that was what was making the noise.

Just then, her friend came in from outdoors. She asked him if he had heard the noisy pickup that had passed.

"No," he replied, "but I do hear the smoke alarm and I believe that your cake is burning!"

He hurried to take care of the smoke detector and Eleanor rushed to tend to her cake. With the smoke settled and her nerves collected, she said, laughing, "Now I know why everyone hurries to turn the smoke alarm off."

Every year, when our sons were little, our family celebrated my birthday at the Minnesota State Fair. We would arrive early in the morning and spend the day. We spent a lot of time touring the animal barns and walking around the midway. I could still hear then and just as the farm sounds frightened me when I stayed on my uncle's farm, they frightened me at the fair. My favorite sound on the midway was the merry-go-round music.

Myron and I continued the tradition after the boys had left home. By then all was silent for me. I could only imagine what it would be like when the sounds were returned to me. I was caught up in the excitement the minute I walked through the gates. I no longer tagged along after Myron. He had a hard time keeping up with me!

The sounds in the barn were awesome. I still did not like the mooing of the cattle but after I heard my first rooster crow, I stood by their pens, begging them to crow some more. The sounds of the midway were exactly as I remembered them, only much louder. I heard the merry-go-round music, the screaming of the riders on the scary rides and the hawkers as we passed by. The sounds did become too loud so I didn't stay long.

I went and sat on the bench at the entrance to the midway where the sound was "just right." The following year, when Myron visited the barns and the midway, I visited the arts and craft building and walked from bandstand to bandstand listening to the music.

My favorite group was West Bound, a country western group whose leader was a member of our church. I hadn't been listening for long when, suddenly, over the loudspeaker, I heard Jeff talking about a woman sitting in the stands who had been deaf and now could hear. I sat up straight. He was talking about me! He told how I had been deaf for 10 years and about the miracle of the cochlear implant. He spoke of how thankful I was to be able to hear his music.

Then, he surprised me by dedicating a song to me that I had not heard in years, "You Are My Sunshine." In no time, everyone was singing along. It was an amazing way to share the wonderful news of the implant—over the loudspeaker system to thousands of people at the State Fair.

The State Fair brought me yet another opportunity to share my story and that opportunity led me to an even bigger way of giving back. In the fall of 1999, while visiting the newly opened University of Minnesota building on the grounds, I saw a poster advertising mini-medical school classes that were going to be held at the university in the fall. They were open to the public on a first-come, first-serve basis. There would be no fees, no tests and the only prerequisite was an inquisitive mind, which I certainly had.

It was not my field of choice. I would much rather be taking a teaching course but I thought this was my chance to attend college. If I attended all the lectures, I would receive a mini-doctor of medicine certificate. I filled out the registration card and placed it in the box on the counter. Then, like many high school seniors, I waited to find out if I was accepted.

I waited and waited and waited. Then, two weeks before classes were to begin, I received a letter of acceptance and welcome. I was going to college! Two lines of the letter stood out above the rest.

"You don't need a scientific background to understand and enjoy mini-medical school. Just bring your curious mind and we'll take care of the rest."

Of the six lectures (anatomy, infectious diseases, physiology, genetics, cancer and complementary care) I attended, it was natural that because of the otosclerosis that ran through my family, it was the lecture on genetics that was most interesting to me. I certainly brought my curious mind with me that evening and I asked many questions. I had always been concerned that our grandchildren might inherit otosclerosis so now I had my chance to find out what a professor would have to tell me.

I asked, "Since our four sons do not have otosclerosis, does it skip generations?"

He couldn't answer my question. I left that evening with more questions than answers and that led me to Dr. Richard Smith at the Molecular Otolaryngology Research Laboratories of the University of Iowa. Dr. Smith is very interested in otosclerosis and was excited about studying the hearing loss in my extended family. The study is called a genetic linkage study. It is hoped that by studying my extended family, scientists will be able to localize the gene or genes causing otosclerosis.

On June 3, 2000, Dr. Smith came to Trinity Lutheran Church in Detroit Lakes, Minnesota to meet with 25 family members who

**Research Group:** *Members of the Tingelstad family pose with Dr. Richard Smith of the University of Iowa, where researchers are looking for the genetic cause of otosclerosis.*

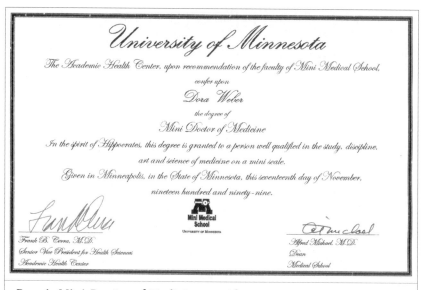

*Dora's Mini-Doctor of Medicine certificate*

had gathered there. While he busied himself conducting hearing tests and taking blood samples, the family visited and shared a potluck meal.

After my book, *Journey Out of Silence*, was published, I received more opportunities to give back what had been given to me. In addition to book signings and readings, I received invitations for speaking engagements at hospitals, schools, libraries and churches. Each was special but there are some that stand out.

My first reading was at the library in my hometown of Pelican Rapids, Minnesota. I read to a full house of relatives, old friends and neighbors who had come to see the hometown girl who had made good. I smile now as I think of that day. I did sign several copies of my book but I wonder why they needed one as I got carried away and practically read the entire book! After that, I decided to stick with telling my story.

*Dora at a book signing of* Journey Out of Silence *at the Pelican Rapids, Minnesota, Public Library*

I did just that when I was invited to be the guest speaker at the Lutheran Women's Missionary League (LWML) Fall Rally in Carver County. Once again, the words flowed and I didn't have any problems hearing the questions that followed.

When Pastor Scott Gustafson, Zone LWML counselor, stood up to give the closing devotion, he tossed his prepared notes aside. He said that, after hearing my presentation, he decided to choose a different Bible passage from John 10, "My sheep hear my voice," on which to speak. Jesus does love us and wants us to share his voice with others—in church, at work, and with family.

My book was also used as a means of promoting health education. I was invited to participate in Open Book: A Minnesota Author Series for Your Health, organized by the Resource Center of Ridgeview Medical Center in Waconia, Minnesota. I also spoke to audiology students of the National Speech Language Hearing Association (NSLHA) at the University of Minnesota. The notes of thanks I received made me feel that the time I spent sharing my story was very important.

Dear Dora,
Thank you for coming to Ridgeview last night to tell your uplifting story. We admire your dedication to educating others about the implant.

Sincerely,<br>Jane

Dora,
Your story was so moving and poignant! Thank you so much for speaking to us. I spoke to students who said that they were even more motivated to become audiologists. Thank you so much for telling us about deafness and hearing.

Diana

Some of my friends and acquaintances began to tease me about becoming famous and I guess, although no one asked me for my autograph, people did begin to recognize me. When that happened, I remembered another little poem that I wrote which I placed at the end of one of my family history writings.

I didn't write for the glory
I didn't write for the fame.
I didn't write to get a big name
I just wrote to tell my story
to record history was my aim.
But if I ever do get famous
I'll try real hard not to complain.

This is as true today as it was when I wrote it but with one very important change. With this book, in addition to encouraging those who are hearing impaired to consider having the cochlear implant, I want to share my experiences with bilateral implants. My most important goal for writing *I Danced* is to inspire others who are experiencing difficulties with their cochlear implant. I do not want them to become discouraged and stop using their cochlear implant. I want them to go that extra mile in hopes that they, too, can continue with their journeys into the wonderful world of sound.

Yes, my life did become very busy and rewarding. One evening, when I was scurrying around getting my things organized for a speaking engagement, Myron asked me, "Do you ever sit still?"

I guess I don't remain still very often because as long as there is an opportunity to help someone hear, I can't just sit. Although I don't handle celebrity status well, I won't complain for that is a very small price to pay for what was given to me. I enjoy every minute of every day and I thank God for giving me this wonderful gift to share.

# A Bell is for Ringing

The medical records of my previous ear surgeries and my MRI prior to my cochlear implant surgery remind me how blessed I am to have a cochlear implant. By the time I was 23 years old, otosclerosis had already done much damage to both my middle and inner ear. A stapes mobilization on my right ear had been unsuccessful in restoring my hearing. A fenestration surgery, also on my right ear, was aborted due to a great amount of calcification.

I underwent an unsuccessful stapedectomy, again on my right ear, in 1972 and a revisal of that stapedectomy in 1985. That also was unsuccessful. Now, here I was 14 years later, hearing wonderfully well with my Nucleus 22 cochlear implant system that had been chosen for me during my surgery.

At the initial cochlear implant evaluation, I was shown the processor of two implants. One was the Clarion model which was not yet approved by the Food & Drug Administration (FDA). The other was the Nucleus 22 which surgeons had been implanting for several years.

I am drawn to simplicity so the Clarion, with the microphone, the transmitter and the magnet all in one piece, appealed to me. I chose the Clarion. Only a few days later, I met my first cochlear implant recipient.

I had started taking my walks to the McDonald's Restaurant in the morning before it got too hot. Not too many are up and around at 6:30 so I had the restaurant all to myself. I was busy writing a letter, oblivious to what was going on. When I looked up, I was surprised to see a man sitting in the booth in front of me. When I looked around and saw that all the other booths were empty, I wondered, *Why, with all the empty booths, did he choose the one in front of me?*

When I saw what I was quite sure was the Nucleus 22 magnet on his head and the microphone over his ear, I knew why. I certainly was not going to let him leave without talking to him.

On the pretense of getting more coffee, I walked up to the counter. I stopped at his booth on the way back and, pointing to his head, I asked, "Is that a cochlear implant?" All he said was, "Yes" so I sat down.

I wasn't finished with him yet. I wrote a note telling him I was going to be implanted. I asked him when and where he had his surgery.

Then he responded!

He had been implanted the previous December. He had chosen the Nucleus 22 as he had just recently lost his hearing. He did not want to wait for the Clarion to be approved by the FDA. I was amazed at how well he could hear. When he showed me his processor and explained how it worked, I was no longer as intimidated and that was reassuring to me.

I stuck with my choice of a Clarion, even after reading the note Myron brought home from work telling of the results of my MRI. When Myron came home that day, I could not read his face and I certainly did not want to read the note. He wasn't about to tell me what it contained so I had no choice but to do so. I didn't get farther than "Left ear is filled with bone, won't work; right ear has fluid and will work," before my eyes filled with tears of thankfulness that rolled down my cheeks. Through the tears, I read the second part.

"It may be possible to have the Clarion Model implanted but won't know for sure until the time of surgery. Both models will be in the operating room."

That part was of no importance to me. All that mattered was that I was going to have a chance to hear again. I was confident that the one implanted would be the one I was to have. Before that could happen, I had to endure one more test, a promontory stimulation test. That would be the deciding factor. If I heard the sounds instead of experiencing a sensation of sound, I would be a candidate.

I remember that day very well. I did not experience any pain when the Novocain was injected, possibly because I was so tense and already felt numb. I had gone through a stapesmobilization, an attempted fenestration and two stapedectomies in that ear, all without success. I wondered how in the world my auditory nerve could still function.

I concentrated on hearing. My auditory nerve was working and I heard! It was not the tinnitus that I heard. I listened to the beeps as they grew louder and then softer sounds I had not heard for more than 15 years. My body relaxed so much that I became weak. When the procedure was finished, I staggered down the hall so giddy with happiness I was bumping into the walls as I followed Myron out into the waiting room.

I was given my surgery date of August 26, just four days before my 58th birthday. Once again, I would receive a wonderful birthday present.

That morning, Myron and I were on our way to the hospital at 4:30 a.m. I was wheeled into the operating room at 7 a.m. Four hours later, I woke up to the gentle touch of the recovery room nurse. I smiled and went back to sleep.

The next time I awoke, my audiologist was in my room explaining to Myron how I came to have the Nucleus 22 implant. She explained that with the Clarion a special tool is needed to insert the electrode into the cochlea. When a dummy wire was inserted, it met a block and the wire bent. My surgeon could not feel if the blockage was difficulty with the wire or a block in my cochlea so he pulled it out and tried the electrode of the Nucleus 22.

The Nucleus 22 electrode is hand-fed into the cochlea so it is easier to feel any resistance. When a block was felt, the wire was moved and full insertion was received. If I had received the Clarion, the wire would have been crimped and only in part way. I would not receive as much information as I would with full insertion of the Nucleus 22 electrode.

I was not at all disappointed. I knew that what I needed, the Nucleus 22, was safely tucked away inside the recesses of my head. In only four weeks, I would find out just how much I did need it.

On the morning of my activation, I was awake early and we arrived at the clinic with time to spare. While we sat waiting, my friend from McDonald's walked in. He didn't stay long, just long enough to wish me luck and then he was off to work in the Cochlear Implant Research Laboratory.

Soon after, my audiologist walked in, her arms laden with boxes. She said, "Let's go," and we followed her into the sound-treated room that I had come to know so well. As she was opening each box and laying the contents on the desk, I had a sinking feeling that she would ask me to assemble them. They looked very complicated to me. Luckily, she did the assembling and when she finished, I was amazed at how compact everything was. It reminded me of a Walkman®.

Then, she proceeded to adjust the outer magnet until

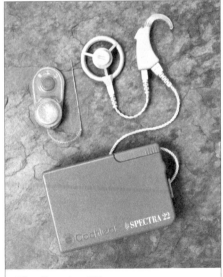

*The Spectra 22*

it grasped the magnet that was implanted inside my skull. She plugged my processor into her computer and said, "Let's get to work."

She handed me this handwritten note, "Don't worry if you don't hear anything right away. It may take five minutes."

It did not take five minutes. I heard a sound immediately. She gave me a questioning look and asked, "Do you hear that?"

I assured her that I did and she began slowly but steadily to increase the loudness until I reached my comfort level. The normal procedure is to go through this with each electrode but she got through only the first six. Then, just as I had been warned, my otosclerosis affected the next eight electrodes. They either caused facial stimulation or made me dizzy and were shut down. Believe me, I was relieved when I was able to take the last six up to my comfort level.

Next, I had to balance the loudness of the electrodes. When this was completed, my processor was unplugged from the computer and a battery was placed in the battery compartment.

She mouthed, "Are you ready?"

I said, "Yes," and with a flip of the switch, I came out of silence. Myron spoke and his voice was exactly as I remembered it to be.

After receiving instructions as to how my processor worked, I was sent out into the world of sound. The waiting room was very noisy, the elevator made a racket and the flushing of the toilet was frighteningly loud. When I stepped outdoors, the sounds of traffic and airplanes flying overhead were so overwhelming that I found myself trying to fend them off as I hurried to our car.

Myron wanted to spend the afternoon with me but he had to return to work. I had so much fun. When I got tired of opening and shutting the cupboard doors to hear the squeaks, running the water in the kitchen sink and listening to our squeaky floors, I moved outdoors. There, I heard the neighbors' lawnmowers, the cars coming up the street and the laughter of the children at the Day Care across the street. There was one persistent sound I heard and could not identify. I found out what it was when I returned to the clinic the following morning.

When my surgeon came into the examining room, he asked if I could hear the birds. I had not expected to be asked that question. I thought for a moment and since it was fall, I answered, "I don't think there are any songbirds still around."

On the ride home, I remembered the persistent sound I had heard the day before and I thought, *That's what it was. It was the birds.*

When our car came to a stop in the garage, I jumped out and hurried to the front lawn and listened. The same sounds were there just as I had heard them the day before. I knew that even though the birds hid from me, I was hearing their songs. I decided to take a walk up to our church. The sounds followed me and became louder and louder as I neared the church. Then, I saw them—a huge flock of blackbirds enjoying their lunch in the churchyard. I have heard many more songs since then but, that day, none could have sounded more beautiful.

When I returned from my visit with the birds, I went out to the mailbox which is at the end of our driveway. A loud car sped by. Coincidence or not, my right eye began to twitch so badly I had to remove my processor.

When Myron came home from work, he found me in tears. He called the clinic and was told to bring me right in. My audiologist was waiting for us when we arrived. She quickly found the guilty electrode and it was deactivated. One more electrode was deactivated a couple of days later. I was then down to 10 active electrodes.

At my three-month cochlear implant follow-up appointment, my sound field testing, using warble tones, showed I had a borderline hearing loss. In speech testing, I scored 86 percent in the everyday sentence test and 44 percent in the one-syllable word test.

At my one year evaluation, my sound field testing, again using warble tones, showed that I had a mild hearing loss. My one-syllable word test score dropped from 44 percent down to 22 percent but my everyday sentence score rose one percent, up to 87 percent.

I am amused when I read the remarks of my audiologist. It is quite apparent she did not think I came in for "tune-ups" often enough. She wrote that I seemed to think if adjustments were made, I would not hear as well. She also wrote that I said I hear "Everything," and was eager to encourage others to take advantage of the procedure. She was correct on all three counts.

I certainly did encourage others to have the cochlear implant. I wanted everyone to be able to hear and I was not in a hurry to be remapped. After all, I could already hear "Everything!" Quite likely, she grew weary of hearing about it as I do remember telling her over and over. For 10 years, I lived in silence, trapped behind a thick, black curtain. At my hookup, the curtain lifted and I was set free. I was back in the wonderful world of sound. Yes, I definitely thought I could hear "Everything!"

I heard the changing sounds of the four seasons in Minnesota. I listened to the honking of the geese as they flew south that fall and a sound I had so dearly missed—the crunch of the fallen leaves under my feet. The songbirds had already migrated south but I heard the raucous cries of the blackbirds and those sounds were music to my ears.

Winter in Minnesota is beautiful and the sounds it brings with it are even more so. The crunch of leaves under my feet gave way to the crunching of snow. I never knew boots could be so noisy until I heard their squeaks as people walked by in the hall outside the cafeteria where I had my morning coffee before going to the cochlear implant research lab. After a good old fashioned snowstorm, the still of the early morning was interrupted with the whirring of a hundred snow blowers.

I regressed back to my childhood that first spring. I wasn't as steady on my feet as I was when I was 10 years old but I could not resist walking across the rubbery ice that formed on the water puddles overnight. Again, I heard the bubbling of the water underneath the ice and the swoosh as it pushed its way up through the cracks in the ice. Resisting my urge to send paper boats sailing down the streams of water from the melting snow, I was entertained by the tinkling music as it flowed down the street and the crescendo as it roared into the storm sewer.

There were so many wonderful sounds to get reacquainted with my first summer. I learned to recognize the songs of the birds that visited our back yard. I heard frogs, crickets and cicadas. I heard the roar of motorboats out on the lakes, the neighbors' lawnmowers, the clicking of the lawn sprinklers and the quiet made when the central air conditioners went off and the "thump" as they came back on.

I was swept up in the excitement of a Minnesota Twins baseball game. I no longer saw the "Star Spangled Banner" being sung. I heard it. I joined the fans as they sang "Take Me Out to the Ballgame" and listened to the crack of the bat and the umpire call S-T-R-I-K-E! And I heard two of the sounds I had missed the most—the roar of a waterfall and the rumble of thunder.

We had taken many trips up the North Shore after I became profoundly deaf and we would always stop at Gooseberry Falls, just north of Duluth, Minnesota. After a winter of lots of snow, it was a beautiful sight to see. But as pretty as it was, I was not content to stand there looking at the water as it cascaded down over the jagged rocks. I wanted to hear it! Instead of accompanying Myron farther up on the trail, I went back down and sat on a bench. The first time we returned after my cochlear implant, I was surprised to hear how loud the roar was. It was deafening, just like the tinnitus I had all my life, but I did not want to leave. Myron had to literally pull me away.

The first summer after I regained my hearing, Mother Nature treated me to a spectacular thunderstorm. It was early in the morning. The thunder, like the waterfall, was so loud that at times it actually was deafening. It momentarily caused my processor to shut down. I loved every minute of it. I have not experienced thunder of that magnitude since.

The most beautiful sounds of all, heard around the world, are the sounds of Christmas. Oh, how beautiful is the ringing of the bells. I began collecting bells before I became profoundly deaf. My favorite one is a little silver bell with these words inscribed on one side, "A bell is not a bell until you ring it."

That first Christmas, when I went shopping, I was greeted by the ringing of a much bigger bell, that of the Salvation Army bell ringer. I didn't hurry past like many shoppers did. I placed a donation in the kettle and stood there mesmerized, listening to the bell and talking to the bell ringer. When I felt cold, I moved into the entranceway of the mall, held the door open a crack and stood and listened some more.

The number of bell ringers has dwindled in the last few years but if they are there, I hear the bell as soon as I get out of the car. I remember that first Christmas and a smile comes to my face. I cannot pass one without putting a donation in the kettle and wishing the bell ringer a "Merry Christmas."

And my bells at home—they are no longer trapped behind glass doors. Now, they are scattered around the house, gathering dust, inviting anyone to ring them. They have, at long last, become bells.

# The Importance of Temporal Bone Study to Cochlear Implantation

*by Sharon DeRosa and Saumil N. Merchant, M.D.*

One of the best ways to learn about hearing disorders is by studying the temporal bone. The human temporal bone is the part of the skull containing the structures of hearing and balance—the middle and inner ears. The inaccessibility of the temporal bone during life has always been a difficult problem for researchers studying hearing disorders. It is only after death that scientists can access the temporal bone to examine the hearing and balance systems. This is one of the key reasons why ear research has progressed more slowly than that of other organs in the human body, as the eye.

The need to balance temporal bone research in the United States has been recognized since the mid 1950s. The National Temporal Bone Banks Program was established by the Deafness Research Foundation and the American Academy of Otolaryngology in 1960 to identify individuals with ear disorders and register those who would pledge their temporal bones at death for scientific research. Over the course of the next 30 years, nearly 6,000 pledges of temporal bones were made through the Temporal Bone Banks Program. During this time, however, the number of active temporal bone collections and investigators declined, and by 1990 there were approximately half the number of active temporal bone laboratories as there were in the mid-1970s.

The National Institute of Deafness and Other Communication Disorders (NIDCD) of the National Institutes of Health recognized this trend and the need to rejuvenate interest in human temporal bone research. In 1992, the NIDCD awarded a contract to the Massachusetts Eye and Ear Infirmary and the Deafness Research Foundation to establish the NIDCD National Temporal Bone, Hearing and Balance Pathology Resource Registry to continue and expand on the activities of the Temporal Bone Banks Program. The Registry not only recruits donors, but also disseminates information about temporal bone donation and research to the public and biomedical community, develops and implements professional education activities, conserves human temporal bone collections which are at risk of being destroyed, and maintains a computerized database of all temporal bone collections in the United States.

All 27 temporal bone laboratories in the United States collaborate with the Registry. The Registry's computerized database contains information on over 12,000 temporal bone specimens currently contained in these collaborating laboratories. Scientists can make use of the database (at no cost) for their research studies. The Registry also encourages human temporal bone professional educational activities and investigative collaboration in the study of hearing and balance disorders. The Registry continues to offer workshops and Travel Fellowships for scientists and clinicians interested in the study of the human auditory and vestibular systems. The workshops carry no registration fees and are designed to provide up-to-date information on a variety of temporal bone techniques and disorders. The Travel Fellowship provides travel funds for research technicians and young investigators to visit a temporal bone laboratory for a brief educational visit, lasting approximately one week. The emphasis is on the training of research assistants, technicians and junior faculty.

The services of the Registry and the thousands of temporal bones in the country's temporal bone collections have became a vital resource for scientists researching hearing and balance disorders. Unfortunately there are still certain otological disorders and conditions that are underrepresented in the collections. Cochlear implants fall into this category. Currently, there are over 22,000 adults and children in the United States that have received cochlear implants, but there are only temporal bones from less than 50 implanted patients in the U.S. temporal bone collections. As a result, research on the effects of cochlear implantation on the human ear have been limited, and there is scarcity of information in the literature.

The value of temporal bone research of cochlear implant users cannot be overstated. In addition to improving our understanding of how the structures of the inner ear are affected by various types of hearing loss, scientists will be able to understand the impact of the cochlear implant on the ear. They will be able to determine whether an implant actually worked the way it was designed to work, whether the implant caused any trauma to the ear, and if there is a better way to design the implant to work more efficiently. The information obtained from this research will help both physicians and their patients make more informed decisions based on a better understanding of the benefits different people get from the implant and what surgical strategies might be used during implantation.

Anyone who is a current cochlear implant user is an ideal candidate to be a donor. If you are interested in learning more about the National Temporal Bone Registry please contact us at the addresses listed below.

NIDCD National Temporal Bone, Hearing and
Balance Pathology Resource Registry
243 Charles Street
Boston, MA 02114-3096
(800) 822-1327 Toll-Free (Voice)

(888) 561-3277 Toll-Free (TTY)
(617) 573-3838 Fax
E-mail: tbregistry@meei.harvard.edu
Website: http://www.tbregistry.org

# Genetic Otosclerosis Linkage Analysis Study

*by Richard Smith, M.D.*

Clinical otosclerosis occurs in 0.2–1 percent of white adults, making it the most common cause of hearing impairment. The disease is characterized by isolated hardening of the bone that surrounds the delicate structures of the inner ear. Hearing loss is heralded by the appearance of areas of hard bone called otosclerotic foci that invade the stapedio-vestibular joint and interfere with motion of the stapes, one of three ossicles that transmit sound pressure waves from the ear drum to the inner ear. The average age-of-onset is in the third decade, and 90 percent of affected persons are under 50 years of age at the time of diagnosis.

In about 10 percent of people with clinically significant otosclerosis, sensorineural hearing loss develops across all frequencies. This loss is caused by either mechanical or toxic damage to the inner ear as otosclerotic foci invade the bone and encroach on the delicate inner ear structures. While the sensorineural component of the hearing loss caused by otosclerosis cannot be corrected,

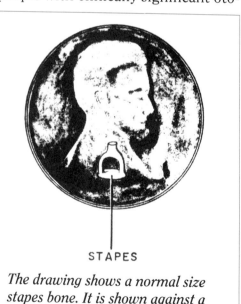

**STAPES**

*The drawing shows a normal size stapes bone. It is shown against a penny for comparable size.*

stapes microsurgery is a highly successful way to restore the normal conduction mechanism and can improve hearing by as much as 50 dB. In studying families like the Tingelstads, we hope to identify genes that lead to otosclerosis. The identification of these genes will aid in our understanding and treatment of this type of hearing loss.

A linkage analysis is a genetic study to localize a particular gene that is segregating (running) in a family. In the study of otosclerosis the gene in question would be the gene or one of the many genes that cause otosclerosis.

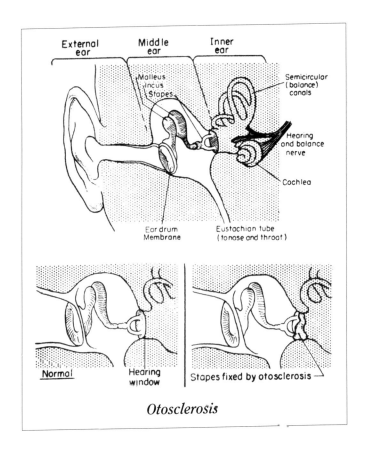

*Otosclerosis*

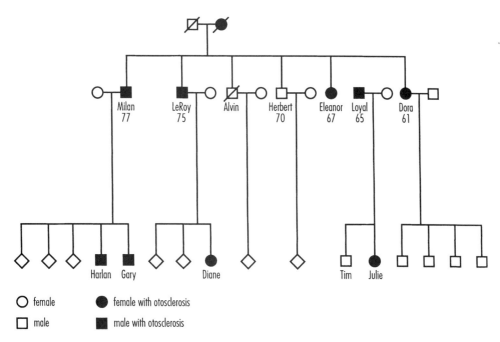

*Pedigree of Dora's Family*

To do a linkage study, it is important to study as many persons in the family with hearing impairment and with normal hearing as possible. It is also important to study their spouses, as it adds valuable information.

Initially, a linkage study entails the construction of a pedigree, indicating individuals with hearing impairment and individuals without hearing impairment. Ideally, the pedigree should be as large as possible, including cousins, nephews, nieces and even distant relatives.

Once the pedigree is constructed, the next step requires obtaining a small blood sample from every person who has a hearing loss in the extended family. DNA is then extracted from the blood, and the DNA is then studied to find areas that are common to all persons with hearing loss. Ideally, it is nice to examine family members in person. If there is a large enough pedigree with enough persons with hearing loss, these areas must contain the gene or genes that cause otosclerosis.

Richard Smith, MD
Sterba Hearing Research Professor and Vice-Chairman,
Department of Otolaryngology-Head and Neck Surgery
Director, Molecular Otolaryngology Research Laboratories

*Dora and her sister Ellie give back "that all may hear."*

"Never place a period where God has placed a comma."

—Gracie Allen

# Part Two

# Traveling On
## 2001-2002

Several times, both in *Journey Out of Silence* and in this writing, I shared with you my childhood dream of becoming a teacher. Had my dream come true, I would have chosen to become an English teacher. Learning the parts of a sentence—nouns, verbs, adjectives, adverbs—came easily to me and diagramming a sentence was like a game.

Of course, punctuation was very important. A period is placed at the end of a statement, an exclamation mark shows excitement and a question mark follows an inquiry. Commas are used to separate a clause within a sentence or to indicate a pause.

I ended the last sentence of my book, *Journey Out of Silence*, with a period. After I had come out of silence, there was a pause—and then my journey continued. Would a comma have been a more appropriate punctuation mark with which to end my book?

# The Missing Puzzle Piece

Since the first week of my activation, when 12 of my electrodes made me dizzy or caused my face to twitch and had to be deactivated, the thought that some day more would have to be turned off was always close to my mind. When I recall some incidents that occurred shortly after the initial stimulation of my electrodes, I can't help but wonder if others were already beginning to cause problems and that they were operating on borrowed time.

The first such incident occurred about two months after my activation. I had been at a craft show in a mall all day. It had been very noisy. That night, I woke up to what was very similar to labor pains—not in my abdomen but in my head. A pinching pain built up. It gradually released its grip, only to build up into more pain. Over and over this happened.

The next day, all was well and there didn't seem to be anything wrong with my hearing but I chose to wear my processor only sparingly. It did not happen that night and it has not happened since but there was another change. I began to experience strange sensations around the site of my receiver. Most days, I enjoyed beautiful hearing but along with it came a feeling of heaviness around the implant site.

I never expected my hearing to go down as long as my 10 electrodes were activated and I cannot recall noticing a change in my hearing. Perhaps, as it happened with my acoustical hearing, it was so gradual that it was not noticeable.

The only problem I had was while watching television. For a time after I received my cochlear implant, I was elated to be able to hear the weatherman without closed captioning. I think this was due to the predictability of common words like rain, wind, humidity, snow, storm, temperature and wind chill that are used frequently during a forecast.

I also understood the speeches of our president and my governor without the help of closed captioning.

Then, for a while, the programs became unpredictable. No matter how much I fiddled with the dials on my processor and the television, the sounds were not clear. Loud, yes, but very unclear.

It reminded me of when I was a little girl helping my brother put a puzzle together. We always started from the border and filled in from there. Soon, there were pockets scattered here and there with one or two missing puzzle pieces. Those were the ones I looked for; I was very proud of myself when I found those pieces. The puzzles my brother chose had many small pieces so it could stay on the card table for days, each day getting prettier and prettier—the picture coming to life.

Then, one day, I would come home from school and find the puzzle was finished except for one gaping hole—a missing puzzle piece. I looked and looked for that puzzle piece without success. I tried to ignore it but I always knew the puzzle would be prettier if that piece were in place.

That is how I felt with the hearing I was receiving with my Nucleus 22 cochlear implant. The picture was pretty. I had a feeling of accomplishment but also a feeling of disappointment that, having spent so much time on mappings, I could not achieve the clear sound I had once experienced. When the opportunity came in a very surprising and unexpected way to improve my hearing, I took it. My journey was going to take me in search of those missing puzzle pieces.

In the summer of 2000, a brochure announcing the FDA approval of the ESPrit 22, an ear level speech processor compatible with my Nucleus 22 cochlear implant, arrived in the mail. I certainly did not expect it to play such an important role in this part of my journey. The illustration certainly was appealing. The speech processor and a built-in microphone were combined in a behind-the-ear (BTE) case.

It looked similar to the BTE hearing aids I had worn for 30 years. I had not reached the point where a body worn hearing aid was recommended. If one had been, I would not have purchased it. I was very vain and ever so careful that my hair covered my hearing aids. Without a doubt, if I had my cochlear implant back then and the ESPrit had become available, I would have been first in line to receive one.

Now that my hearing was restored after having spent 10 years in total silence, it did not concern me if my transmitting cable hung on my neck or there was a bulge where I carried my speech processor in my shirt pocket. I was so thankful for my wonderful hearing, I would have pulled my processor behind me in a wagon. I wasn't at all embarrassed by it. If I noticed someone staring at it, I took the opportunity to explain what it was.

Little by little, I became drawn to the little ESPrit. My friends began getting it and they wrote glowingly of how well they could hear with it and how nice it was to be free of the long cable. I also read the testimonials of others that appeared in "Soundings," a Cochlear Corporation (now Cochlear Americas) publication. What interested me the most was that others were hearing well with their ESPrits and that there were programs from which to choose. The freedom I would receive without the cable hanging down my neck did begin to interest me but for a more practical reason than vanity.

Once again, just as when I went looking for help for my deafness, it was my grandchildren who played a role in my decision. This time it was my youngest two, Brandon and Ashley. I submitted my reason for wanting the ESPrit 22 to "Soundings." The article appeared in the Summer 2000 issue.

## My Grandchildren—My Motivation

In September 1996, after a lifetime of hearing impairment that led to 10 years of deafness, my Nucleus 22 cochlear implant was activated and I re-entered the wonderful world of sound. My motivation then was to hear my grandchildren and to talk to them. I cannot begin to express the joy and thankfulness when I hear, "Grandma! Grandma!" as they come through the door. Since my hookup, three more grandchildren have joined the family and, once again, I was able to hear the most beautiful sound in the world—that of a newborn baby crying. They cried without tears while mine flowed freely.

Today, I am contemplating purchasing the ESPrit 22 and I ask myself, "Why do I want it?" The answer comes loud and clear. Once again, my grandchildren are my motivation! They quickly spy that strange thing hanging down Grandma's neck. Quick as a flash, up comes a hand and the cable is securely clasped in an ironclad fist.

Down comes the headset! Out goes an SOS and Mom has to come to my rescue. After I receive my ESPrit 22, they will, once again, have to be content to go for Grandma's glasses.

Thus it was that I found myself filling out an application form, placing it in an envelope, addressing it to my health insurance provider and dropping it in the mailbox. Then, I sat back and waited. I waited and waited. Finally, one day the familiar looking envelope was there.

I couldn't wait until I got into the house to read it. I ripped it open and read the letter as I walked up the driveway. It wasn't the reply I had been looking for; I was very disappointed. My request was denied.

The following Monday, when I was at the clinic for my weekly research session, I told my audiologist the bad news. There was still hope that I might be able to get one. She offered to write a letter of appeal and asked me to bring the letter of predetermination with me the following week.

It was several weeks before I had a chance to talk to my audiologist again. One day as I rounded the corner on my way to the research lab, I found her office door open and I peeked in. She was standing by her desk, sifting through a pyramid of papers. She looked up, smiled and said, "Hi!"

I took the letter out of my bag and handed it to her. The next few minutes was like something out of the twilight zone. She only had time to glance at it before I heard myself say, "I would rather have another implant."

Where those words came from, I do not know. I had heard the phrase "Those words were put in my mouth," many times but I had always received them with a grain of salt. In fact, I was very skeptical. Now, here I was, experiencing that phenomenon. I had not been consciously thinking about bilateral implants for myself.

I had read an article in our CIAI newsletter so I knew about the clinical bilateral study being conducted at the University of Iowa. I didn't think about it other than to wonder what it would sound like to have two. I knew it was impossible for me to be a candidate. My right ear was chosen for my first implant because my left ear was too calcified. I had surprised myself when I said those words but I was equally surprised with the reply I received from my audiologist.

She didn't seem to think I had said anything out of the ordinary. It seemed as though everything was rehearsed and we were reading from a script. She looked up at me, a serious look on her face, and said, "If you do, you have to talk to your doctor."

I didn't waste any time. Placing the letter back inside my bag, I hurried to the appointment desk and asked for the earliest appointment. When asked for the reason for my visit, I replied, "To talk about having another implant."

There was one other person I had to talk with about it, Myron. I couldn't wait to do so! I wondered what his reaction would be and knew he would be surprised. I had never indicated a wish for bilaterals to him. I didn't think he even knew what bilateral implants were. What would he say about all this? Would he be willing to travel along with me?

# Now What?

When I was at the Clinical Phychoacoustics Laboratory for my weekly research session, I had the opportunity to meet patients, young and old, who had come to the Cochlear Implant Clinic hoping to receive better hearing. Quite often they had not met anyone who had an implant.

I was frequently asked by an audiologist to visit with them. I would show them the external parts of my implant: the processor, the microphone and the most intriguing of all, the magnet. Many were amazed that by placing it on my head, I could hear. I would let them feel the area if they wished. Many were awed by the fact that there were no plugs or wires through the skin. Then I would do my best to explain how everything worked together to give me sound.

It was a fun experience to see how the patients reacted and to see the look of hope that came to their faces, and those of their loved ones, as we visited.

I also received other requests. I was asked to trouble shoot the Nucleus 22 processors that patients were having problems with and sometimes I would be used as a sounding board. My MAP would be programmed into that of another's processor to see if it sounded OK to me.

MAP is the pathway to hearing, the way a processor's parameters are set to deliver sound.

While I was at the clinic, I often received invitations to assist the audiologists with the Lions' 5-M tours through the audiology clinic or to share my story at a Lions' 5-M function. I was happy and proud to assist the cochlear implant team in any way I could.

The favors I did for them were small compared to the gift they had given to me.

It wasn't often, when Myron picked me up at the end of the day, that I didn't have something to share with him. When he first began picking me up, we would greet each other with "How was your day?"

His answer rarely changed. It was always, "The same."

I so often had something to share with him that soon, when I hopped in the car, he began to ask me, "What did you do today?"

He was as thrilled as I was with the changes that my cochlear implant had brought to my life. Nothing surprised him, either. He had come to expect the unexpected. This day, though, what I had to tell him was a bit too much for even him to grasp!

I must have looked like a cat that had just swallowed a canary because when I got into the car that day, he didn't say, "What did you do today?" but asked, "Now what?"

When I said, "I made an appointment to talk about having another implant," Myron didn't say a word. He looked straight ahead. The silence was reminiscent of the day we went seeking information about having my first implant. Only this time, we weren't in complete harmony. He questioned me.

He asked, "Why do you want to do that? You can already hear with the one you have."

I didn't have an answer for him. We drove home in silence that day.

I wanted to know what my sons would think about my having another implant. I chose Scott, our youngest, first. He is the most interested in technology. I was confident he would want me to take advantage of more advanced technology if it became available. I was correct.

Next, I approached Kenny and Dave. They, too, wanted me to go ahead. They were happy with how well I could already hear but,

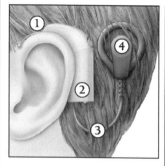
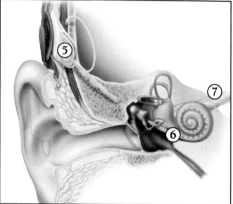

*Pictures courtesy of Cochlear Ltd.*

**The Nucleus® cochlear implant system works in the following manner:**

1. Sounds are picked up by the small, directional microphone located in the ear level processor.

2. The speech processor filters, analyzes and digitizes the sound into coded signals.

3. The coded signals are sent from the speech processor to the transmitting coil.

4. The transmitting coil sends the coded signals as FM radio signals to the cochlear implant under the skin.

5. The cochlear implant delivers the appropriate electrical energy to the array of electrodes which has been inserted into the cochlea.

6. The electrodes along the array stimulate the remaining auditory nerve fibers in the cochlea.

7. The resulting electrical sound information is sent through the auditory system to the brain for interpretation.

if with two implants, I could hear even better, then they wanted me to "Go for it!"

I left our oldest son, Chuck, for last. He absolutely hates hospitals.

I expected him to say, "Mom, you can hear just fine the way you are."

But he surprised me. He smiled and gave me one of his famous hugs and said, "If that's what you want to do, then do it!"

I also began to confide in others but only a few. And then, when they, like Myron, asked why I would want to put myself through the risks of surgery once again, I kept it to myself. I did not know how to answer them. I certainly did have faith that God would again guide my surgeon's hands but I began asking myself the same question. Why did I want another implant? My answer would come by piecemeal in the following weeks.

# Just Do It!

The four-year speech evaluation with my Nucleus 22 cochlear implant and my doctor's appointment were on the same day. My evaluation was in the morning. Before the tests began, my audiologist and I spent some time discussing a second implant.

Just as with my first implant, there was no guarantee that a second would be successful. I was cautioned about the condition of my cochlea. I was reminded that my right ear had been chosen for my first implant because it was the least calcified of the two. The calcification in my left cochlea might make it impossible to get full insertion of the electrode array.

I was aware that the new system of the Cochlear Corporation, named the Nucleus 24, had become available in 1998, two years after my Nucleus 22 was implanted. I assumed it would be the system I would have implanted now. I had done well with the speech coding strategy, called Spectral Peaks (SPEAK), that is on my Nucleus 22.

With the speech coding strategies called Continuous Interleaved Sampling (CIS) or Advance Combination Encoders (ACE) that the Nucleus 24 offered, I would have customized sound. I had briefly examined the processor and it did look more complicated than my Nucleus 22 but I was confident I could learn to operate it. I would make sure to tell Myron to pay attention on the day of my activation.

After we finished chatting, it was time to get to work on my evaluation. I was placed in a chair in front of the speaker. My audiologist went out into the controls room and returned after a short while, a frown on her face. She told me I was not doing well and gave me the choice of continuing on with the evaluation or being reprogrammed. I chose to be reprogrammed. I would return in a few weeks and try again.

My appointment with my doctor was at the end of the afternoon. The risks of surgery, such as short and long-term balance problems, a loss of my sense of taste and temporary or permanent facial paralysis should the facial nerve be severed, remained the same. Even though I did not experience any complications after my first surgery, he said it could occur with this surgery. I would need to have another CT Scan which would show if any changes had occurred in my inner ear in the last three years.

When I was asked if I was sure I wanted to have a second implant, I answered, "Yes." After a surgery date of November 13 was scheduled, I thought that would be the extent of my evaluation.

My audiologist wasn't in quite as big a hurry. There was more work that needed to be done. I would not need to undergo the extensive audiology tests again because she already knew I was deaf. I would, however, need to have an evaluation of my hearing with my Nucleus 22.

Again, I needed to meet with a psychologist. Fortunately, it was with the same doctor I had visited before my Nucleus 22 was implanted. I thought I would breeze right in and out of his office. I was wrong. One session stretched into three.

I was given much to think about between sessions. He must have thought my hearing was good the way it was as he asked me the same question others had asked.

"Why do you want to go through the risks of surgery if only to gain minimal improvement?"

He also brought up the point that if bilateral implants became more common, insurance companies might begin to refuse to cover all cochlear implants. This caused me to pause and think, *Did I want to keep others from experiencing the joy of hearing?*

This question was answered by my doctor at my next appointment and also by my audiologist when I returned for my fourth year evaluation of my Nucleus 22. There was a significant drop in both my sentence and word comprehension scores from those of the previous year. In 1999, I heard 79 percent of the sentences correctly and 44 percent of the words. My scores now were 58 percent and 22 percent respectively.

I also learned at this appointment that Cochlear Americas' new system, called the Nucleus 24 Contour, was soon to be approved by the FDA. We decided to wait for that approval before seeking permission for my second implant from our insurance provider.

The date of my surgery was moved ahead to February 5, one day after our 40th wedding anniversary. The celebration our children planned was put on hold. We would celebrate my improved hearing and our anniversary in the spring.

One day, while chatting with my audiologist, she brought up the subject of my facial nerve. Again, she reminded me of its close proximity to my cochlea. I had not been concerned about this as my first surgery was successful and I was confident that a second would be also.

But then I began to wonder if my CT scan showed that my facial nerve on my left side was closer to the cochlea than it was on my right side. I would remember to talk about this at my next appointment with my doctor.

This and the question of how much hearing gain I might receive were answered. The reason I was having a second implant was to improve my hearing. Since I was still receiving information with my Nucleus 22, my doctor chose to save it.

When I asked him if the facial nerve on my left side was closer to my cochlea than it was on my right side, my doctor smiled and shook his head, "No." Quite likely he sensed my indecisiveness. He looked at me and said, "Just do it!"

I had to come to terms on my own about the insurance question and it did trouble me to the point of keeping me awake at night. It did not help me, either, that during this time I spoke with several patients who were, in their opinions, not doing well with their implants.

I really did not know what to tell my psychologist until, one night, I woke up from a sound sleep. I was wide awake and, like the words, "I would rather have another implant," had been put in my mouth, the thought *these are the people who may be helped by my having another implant* was put in my mind. From that day on, I had no doubt that I was doing the right thing. Now that I had things straightened out in my own mind, I did not have any problems convincing him. My third session was cut short. We shook hands and he wished me luck.

The Nucleus 24 Contour was approved by the FDA a few weeks later. Approval for implant surgery was received and my surgery date was scheduled for January 22, 2001, the birthday of our son, Ken.

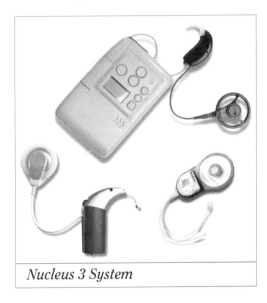

*Nucleus 3 System*

# Very Important Processor

I didn't get many hours of sleep the night before my surgery, perhaps due to my eagerness to have it behind me. I became very sleepy while I was in the preinduction room and had all I could do to keep my eyes open.

I wanted to be awake when Pastor Paul Strawn came to give me a prayerful sendoff to the operating room.

Pastor Strawn had come to serve our church, Prince of Peace Lutheran, in September, only six months before my second implant. He is the same age as our son, Kenny, so it took some time getting used to being ministered to by someone so young. On the other hand, he grew up in the age of technology. Although he had not met anyone with the cochlear implant, he was familiar with the technology.

I had kept in close contact with Pastor Galchutt, our former pastor, after my first implant and he was very excited and happy that I was given the opportunity to receive a second. As he did on my first surgery, he offered to be with me. For a time, I thought both Pastor Strawn and Pastor Galchutt would be with Myron and me before my surgery but that was worked out. Pastor Strawn would visit with us before I went into surgery and Pastor Galchutt would check on me when my surgery was over.

I managed to be awake for Pastor Strawn's visit. It was so comforting to hear the words of his prayer as I had been unable to hear a word as Pastor Galchutt prayed four years before.

I did remember Pastor Galchutt's advice which he had written for me at that time. "Regress back in time and pretend that you are a little girl and you are taking a nap for your mother."

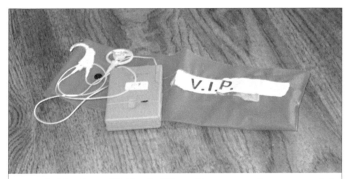

*Dora's Nucleus 22 Body Worn Processor has a special place in her heart.*

That was made so easy to do as after my intravenous was hooked up, I was kept warm with a heated blanket. When one cooled off, another was put in its place.

By the time my audiologist came to the room, I was going in and out of sleep and had a hard time conversing with her. I remember her telling me I could wear my processor into the operating room and keep it on until I went to sleep. She did not know what she would do with it then to ensure that it would be safe.

Just before I left for the operating room, she came up with an innovative idea. She placed a VIP sticker on my Dry Aid bag, the plastic bag I keep my processor in overnight. Then she taped it to the pole that held my intravenous bag. That done, I gave in and fell asleep, only to be awakened again to receive a sendoff kiss from Myron.

About the only thing I remember while in the operating room was my audiologist taking my Nucleus 22 processor off and the black mask coming down over my face. I recall thinking, *Will I ever go to sleep?* I did and it seemed I had been asleep only minutes before awakening to the gentle touch of a nurse.

"You did great," the nurse told me. "We are taking you up to your room now."

I felt very well; I did not have any pain. I wasn't nauseous or dizzy and I did not have the metallic taste I had after my first implant surgery.

Two things needed to be checked out when I reached my room. I looked to see what time it was and I listened for my tinnitus. It was late afternoon so I knew I had not been wheeled in and right out of the operating room as I had been when I was admitted for a fenestration surgery several years before. That was confirmed when I saw Myron standing by my bed, a smile on his face. He told me that surgery was successful.

Just as it had happened after my Nucleus 22 was implanted, my tinnitus was quiet. In fact, all was quiet. The turban I wore on my head prevented me from wearing my Nucleus 22.

When Pastor Galchutt visited me in the early evening, we once again had to resort to communicating by writing notes. I did not like the silence and wanted the night to pass quickly. I had another restless night and thought morning would never arrive. I was relieved when I looked out the window and saw the early morning light.

It was very early when several residents came and proceeded to remove my turban. I had not been thinking about my Nucleus 22 processor so I was surprised when I was asked where it was. I did not know so they went searching and found it safely tucked inside the red plastic Dry Aid bag on a shelf in my closet. With the crew looking on, I put it in place and was back in the wonderful world of sound. Smiles were exchanged as I easily answered questions.

My bed was shielded from the hallway by a curtain so the sounds I heard and recognized were those that were in my room. A banging and clanging sound I thought were construction sounds came repeatedly from the corridor. Finally, my curiosity got the best of me and I asked my nurse if there were workmen near by. She looked at me strangely and said, "No."

She pulled the curtain back when I asked her to and it didn't take long to discover the source of the clanging sound. It was made when metal clipboards that held the patients' records were taken out and replaced in the racks outside the rooms. This may not have been a pleasant sound to others but it certainly was to me. Never, after my other surgeries, had I been able to hear that sound.

My Nucleus 22 processor was not alone in receiving VIP care. All morning, I had my own private nurse. A wonderful nurse-in-training, one of many "angels" I encountered on my journey, was assigned to watch over me. Not only did she check and recheck my vital signs, she assisted me with my morning bath, gave me a massage and, wonder of wonders, shampooed my hair. A shower cap, filled with warm, soapy water, was placed ever so carefully on my head so as not to get my incision wet. Then, it was gently massaged into my hair. When I was released after lunch, the only clue that I had been in the hospital was the wheelchair I rode in.

When we arrived home, I experienced a strange sensation. It brought back memories of my revisal stapedectomy I underwent at the Mayo Clinic in 1985. Even though Dr. McDonald, my surgeon, told me then that the procedure was unsuccessful, I knew I could hear better so I argued with him. When he told me it would be impossible to do so, I asked, "Then, do our ears work independently of each other? Is it possible the hearing in my other ear has improved?"

He replied, "We don't know that."

This time, it was not actual words but whenever Myron spoke, I heard a high-pitched squeal in my newly implanted ear. The squeal was even louder when I flushed the toilet or ran water. It was so irritating when I was talking on the telephone that I had to turn the sensitivity down to Number One. When I went to have my incision checked, I shared this with my doctor and he thought for a long time. He did not have an explanation for it.

I received an unexpected request that day. Since the clinic was embarking on their initial surgery with the Nucleus 24 Contour Implant System, it was given the opportunity to generate awareness of the center as well as to help identify appropriate implant candidates. Would I be willing to be interviewed by the media and possibly have my initial stimulation filmed by local TV stations and aired on prime time newscasts?

I was uncertain at first. Then, as I read the letter requesting the participation of the clinic and saw that the awareness would be directed toward the clinic and the new technology of the Nucleus 24 Contour cochlear implant, I decided to give my consent. What stood out above all else was the chance to bring awareness to others who might benefit from a cochlear implant. My activation day was scheduled for February 15, only two weeks away.

# Giddy as a Kid

There were more things that needed to be done before my activation day which left me with less time to dwell on what my activation would be like. The two weeks went by rapidly.

At the clinic, it was the practice to stimulate some of the electrodes before the initial stimulation. This was to be done on the day I returned to have the staples removed from my incision. That day, the site was found to be swollen so the stimulation had to be postponed.

I had an appointment scheduled a week later to have my Nucleus 22 processor reprogrammed and so the stimulation was done at that time. After not hearing sounds with that ear for possibly 20 years, it was indeed gratifying to hear the familiar "beep, beep, beep" I had heard when my Nucleus 22 was remapped. The sound was clear and true.

A few weeks before my surgery, I had started a research project using my Nucleus 22 that did not get finished so I returned to the Clinical Psychoacoustics Laboratory for several sessions. I did not know then that it would be the last project I would participate in using my Nucleus 22. I quickly learned what it is like to be involved in a media alert.

It was an exciting two weeks. Ms. Kelly Laban of Kovak-Likly Communications, Wilton, Conn. interviewed me by telephone. When I told her I had been sequentially implanted with my Nucleus 24 Contour Implant System, she was very surprised. Now there were two focal points. I had received the latest cochlear implant technology and I was one of a few in the world to be bilaterally implanted.

I had not yet begun using e-mail so Ms. Laban faxed the draft of the interview to Myron at work. Several drafts were faxed back and forth. When the kinks had been ironed out, the interview read:

### About Dora Weber

Dora Weber, 62, of Spring Lake Park, is a mother of four and grandmother of six. Weber first experienced difficulty hearing at age 12. In 1986 she went completely deaf and received her first implant, the Nucleus 22. Shortly after receiving the Nucleus 22, she authored a book chronicling her experience. Since then, Weber has spoken at hospitals, libraries and churches, as well as other venues. She volunteers her time at the Fairview-University Medical Center in the pediatric clinic reading to children who are waiting to see their doctors. In her spare time she sits in the waiting room and speaks to those waiting for their evaluations.

Weber inherited her deafness from her parents who had otosclerosis (spongy growth in the middle ear that causes progressively increasing deafness), as did five of her seven brothers and sisters. Weber began losing her hearing at age 12 and began a series of surgeries at age 19. Surgeries on her left ear were always successful; surgeries on her right ear were always failures. Eventually, Weber's otosclerosis progressed and invaded the cochlea, rendering traditional surgeries ineffective. Weber had some knowledge of cochlear implants, but did not think they were for her.

Weber became frustrated by her constant struggle to understand the words of those around her. Weber's decision to return to the hearing world came one day when she was watching her grandson, Jeffery. She asked him if he would like to have a picnic but could not understand his reply. He repeated himself many times before showing her a coupon for the restaurant he wanted to go to. At that moment, Weber decided she wanted to hear her grandchildren and would pursue whatever avenue needed to achieve that goal. Soon after, Weber was implanted with the Nucleus 22. Now, with the addition of the Nucleus 24 Contour, Weber hopes to gain a greater and richer range of hearing and fully experience the joys of her life.

Kovak-Likly then distributed the interview, along with the time and place of my activation, to regional media, inviting them to witness my activation and to interview me.

As the day of my activation drew closer, I began to wonder how I would carry two body processors. I had purchased pocket T-shirts in every color available before my Nucleus 22 was activated. Over these, I wore short-sleeved button-down blouses in the summer. In the winter, I wore long-sleeved blouses with one breast pocket and wore a vest over them. What would I do with another processor? Simple, I would purchase blouses that had two breast pockets. When I went shopping, I found that blouses with two pockets were not easy to find. I scoured many stores and looked through countless clothes racks before finding two, one yellow and one blue. Then, I was all set.

I would not know until the morning of my activation if the media alert had spurred any interest in my story. I didn't have many birthday parties while growing up but I do remember those I did have. After the invitations were delivered, I would always wonder if anyone would come to the party. This was one "party" when I would not be disappointed if no one showed up. My public speaking had given me experience with the public but certainly not with the media. Television broadcasting was out of my realm. If no one came, it would be just fine with me.

The night before my activation, I had two dreams. One was that I could hear so well with my Nucleus 22 and Nucleus 24 Contour together that I left some hearing in the sound-treated room to share with others. The other was that a receiver stimulator had slipped down into my neck.

I did not have any trouble interpreting the first dream. I knew I would share my story in the hope that others, like myself, could hear. I didn't attempt to interpret the second dream. It was just another of many dreams that were just plain silly. Almost three years later, I found out that it did not need an interpretation. It would come very close to coming true.

My appointment was at 9 a.m. I wasn't as anxious to get to the clinic as I had been the morning of the activation of my Nucleus 22. I am sure the reason for that was because I could already hear. Four years before, I was deaf and looking forward so much to hearing. I couldn't wait to get there and we arrived with plenty of time to spare. This morning we got our coats hung up and only had a few minutes to relax before the show was on the road.

Myron and I were just seated when I looked down the hall which led from the elevators. I saw two young men, one toting a camera, come walking toward us. When I saw the insignia, "Channel 11," printed on their jackets, I nudged Myron and said, "Look who just came!"

Then, like the times when I would get myself in a tight spot by forging ahead without thinking about the consequences, I wondered, *What have I gotten myself into?* I certainly did not know how to act in front of a television camera. Just as it happens when I step up to a podium and begin to speak, the blood rushed to my face. At least, when I give a presentation, I have a script to follow. This time, there would be none. Everything would be ad lib. I certainly was not calm when the crew came over to introduce themselves and to meet us.

This was one time when I did not want to be surrounded by strangers. When my audiologist came into the clinic reception room accompanied by Leigh Anne Monthey, a Senior Clinical Applications Specialist with Cochlear Americas I was acquainted with, I felt a bit more relaxed. When Bob Nemeth, chair of the Lions 5M International Hearing Foundation, walked in, I thought, *Wow! Lots of people have accepted the invitation.* Then, I got to wondering, *How will everyone fit into the small sound-treated room?*

There was standing room only. Myron and Bob Nemeth sat on chairs placed along the wall and the TV crew was stationed in the controls room. My audiologist was seated by the computer. Leigh Anne Monthey stood behind her so she could view the computer. My audiologist had just finished connecting the transmission magnet to the receiver magnet and was about to begin the activation process when she smiled and mouthed the words, "Channel 5 just walked in." That crew joined the group in the controls room.

I was hooked up to the computer so I couldn't even turn around to see them. I had to wait until they came up in front to film. The filming process was handled quite efficiently. First, one camera man would come up to the front of the room and film for a few minutes. He would retreat to the back of the room and the other camera man would come up. There was one thing for certain. The film clips would not be identical.

Even though my processor was different than that of my Nucleus 22, the activation procedure had not changed. Once again, after my threshold levels were found, I took the electrodes up the scale to my comfort level. I did not hear my bull frog, nor a fog horn, like I had heard with my Nucleus 22. The electrodes rang clear and true. All the while, as I waited for this day, I had not concerned myself with the thought that any electrodes would cause facial stimulation.

By the time I remembered about the 10 electrodes that caused facial stimulation at the activation of my Nucleus 22, I had safely taken 13 electrodes up to my comfort level. I was quite confident, then, that we would get through the remaining electrodes and I was just about to mention this to my audiologist when it happened.

As I brought electrode number 14 up the scale, my eye began to twitch. This happened with the next electrode and the next. I brought the remaining six electrodes up to my comfort level. Only three electrodes were deactivated.

After I had balanced the electrodes according to loudness, I was asked, "Do you want to hear voices?"

I said, "Yes!"

I was told to put the batteries in my processor; my audiologist pressed the on/off button and I was on the air. I did hear voices but they sounded muffled. After adjustments were made, sounds were louder but my voice wasn't near as loud as it had been at the activation of my Nucleus 22. That morning, I turned around, thinking that someone else had come into the room.

This morning, I looked behind me to see what was making the terrible high pitched sound I was hearing. When I told my audiologist what I was hearing, she laughed and said, "What you are hearing are the high pitches, like the "S" sound, that you have not heard for many years."

I knew I would not be going home wearing both processors. I needed to try all three speech strategies, SPEAK, ACE and CIS on my Nucleus 24 Contour and then decide which one I liked best before I could begin to use both processors together. I was caught off guard when she asked me, "Do you want to try both devices together?"

I don't think it had ever taken as long to put my magnet in place and the earpiece over my ear as it did that morning. My hands shook badly. This was of benefit to the cameramen as they had time to scurry to the front of the room to get the best vantage point for filming. When I watch the tape of the newscast, I have to smile as the camera of the other is caught in the filming. This was the only filming that was alike on both news broadcasts.

When I finally had everything in place, I said, "I'm on."

My audiologist said, "You are now hearing on both sides of your head."

I sat there too stunned to say anything.

She asked, "What does it sound like?" I answered "It sounds beautiful!"

I could hear the surprise in her voice when she inquired, "It sounds beautiful?"

"It sounds beautiful! I'm hearing on both sides of my head, not just on one side. Everything is just great!" I answered with assurance.

I became overwhelmed and for a few minutes, I was oblivious to any filming that was being done.

I was asked several times if my activation was rehearsed and that made me smile and I felt a bit haughty. I acted spontaneously. No amount of rehearsing could have prepared me for what happened that morning. KARE 11 news anchor, Paul Magers, could not have captured it better with the words he used to lead into the news spot.

"A 62-year-old woman is as giddy as a kid and who can blame her? Technology has returned sweet sounds to Dora Weber's life after a decade of deafness!"

Harris Faulkner, KSTP Channel 5 news anchor, could not have chosen a more descriptive way to end that channel's news clip than with the words, "Quite an amazing thing to witness. Someone who was once deaf, now hearing again. How about that?"

Channel 11 news reporters were finished with filming at noon. Channel 5 wanted to return in the afternoon to film a mock session

*Television news stories featuring Dora's activation. Clockwise from top left: Paul Magers' introduction; audiologist Leigh Anne Monthey; Myron; Dora; testing the device; the receiver of the device*

when I read to the children in the Pediatric Clinic. I was to meet the cameraman in the hospital lobby after lunch. I spent the hour listening to the sounds around me.

I went to the Outside Inn Restaurant for lunch and found the sounds of the dishes clattering, ice falling from the ice machines, people talking and laughing, the cash machines opening and closing and money being exchanged, unbearably loud. As soon as I paid for my lunch, I set my tray down on the nearest counter and turned off my Nucleus 24 Contour. When I sat down, I began adjusting the settings. I hadn't had any help with this so I just turned down both the volume and sensitivity settings until the sounds were bearable.

Then, I soaked up all the sounds! Everything sounded much the same as it did with my Nucleus 22. The noticeable change was that I was hearing with both ears which gave me a feeling of being balanced. It was a wonderful feeling!

After I finished lunch, I walked through the tunnel to the hospital. I was aware of every little sound along the way. Not only could I feel the breeze, I heard it. It was much easier to hear and catch phrases of those who passed by. I could even hear voices of the people who were walking behind me. Once I heard women's voices coming from behind me and I thought that, at any minute, they would pass me. This didn't happen so I turned around to see just where they were. I was very surprised to see the group of ladies was quite a distance behind me. *Wow,* I thought, *I sure am going to like having surround sound!*

It was getting close to the time when I was to meet the Channel 5 cameraman so I went and sat in the hospital lobby. As soon as I sat down, I heard a high pitched "ping." It went away only to return over and over. I tried without success to find the source.

When the cameraman came, we chatted for awhile. All the while, I was hearing this annoying sound. Finally, I just had to know what it was so I asked him. Even he couldn't pinpoint the source without my help. He told me to tell him when I heard it. Then he would look around. Finally, after the third time, he smiled and said, "It is the sound of the keys of the cash register, over at the coffee stand, when they are punched."

Then, we went to the Pediatric Clinic. While the cameras followed me, I set up the easel, organized my books, and sat down to read. The only patients in the clinic were two sisters. The book they picked out was *The Adventures of Corduroy.* To test my hearing, I asked them questions about the story. I heard their answers clearly.

By the time I put the easel and books away, it was time to hurry back to the Cochlear Implant Clinic. It had been a busy and exciting day. I couldn't wait to get home to see the fruits of their labor.

Before I could leave, I had to do something that made me feel very sad. I had to part with my Nucleus 22. I found my audiologist in the sound treated room. I did not linger there for long. I took my Nucleus 22 off, put it in the red plastic Dry Aid kit, the VIP sticker still intact. I handed it to her and said, "Take good care of it. It is a good friend." She assured me that she would.

I turned and walked away. I did not think, then, that when I put it on two months later, the sound would be distorted and would remain so for the next two years.

My hearing on the drive home was not as sharp as it had been after the activation of my Nucleus 22 but I did not have to use the lapel microphone. We arrived home with little time to spare before the Channel 5 five o'clock news began. Myron called our sons and asked them to tape the segment. He also called a few relatives and friends. Some already knew my activation was to be televised since the TV channels had been airing previews of the story during the afternoon hours.

It was a humbling experience to watch the miracle unfold. When I read along with the closed captioning and saw the words, "A once empty glass made half full is now overflowing," the Channel 11 news reporter Marla Matthews spoke, I remembered the dream I had the night before—a dream that had come true.

As soon as the newscast was over, the phone began to ring. Friends, old and new, called with good wishes. My telephone adapter was not yet ready to use so Myron took all the calls. While he chatted, I spent the hour waiting for the Channel 11 six o'clock news by checking out my Jim Reeves CD. The accompanying music was great but the sound of Jim's voice made me laugh. He was singing in monotone. I checked out Johnny Cash and Montana Slim. They, too, were singing way off key.

After watching the nine o'clock segment on Channel 45, Channel 5's sister station, I crawled into bed. I was exhausted but the excitement of the day would not leave me and I lay awake until the early hours of the morning.

I had been given a gift four years ago. That day, I received another gift. I didn't know how I would ever repay it.

# Kaleidoscope of Sounds

*My Journal*

Thursday, February 15—It was much too cold this morning to walk to McDonald's to let my friends know how my activation went. It was quiet in the house so just to hear sounds, I turned on the television. I was surprised to be able to understand some of what was said without using closed captioning. I also checked to see if Jim Reeves had recovered his voice. This time, instead of listening to my boom box, I put the CD on the stereo in our living room. There was a little improvement.

Pastor Paul Strawn came at 10 o'clock. I didn't know if I would hear the doorbell ring so I kept an eye on the driveway. I did hear the doorbell when he rang it but perhaps it was because I was waiting for it to ring. When I opened the door and heard him ask, "How are you doing?" I started to laugh. His voice had changed, too! He has a terrific sense of humor. He asked, "You mean I don't sound like Clark Gable anymore?" As I showed him the processor and switched to the different programs, he would say, "This is just a test" or "Testing—1-2-3." It was a fun visit.

Just as he was getting ready to leave, my daughter-in-law, Sharon, and grandsons, Jeffery and Justin, came. It took some time to adjust to their voices but after awhile, they sounded like I remembered. I hadn't yet been in a different environment so we went to McDonald's for lunch. The noise was loud but bearable in the playroom. I didn't do any adjusting then but when I got home, I just about drove myself up the wall. I changed everything. I became so confused that I almost sent an SOS to my audiologist. But instead, I took out my user manual and read.

### Resetting the Speech Processor

To return the speech processor to the settings pro-grammed by your clinician:
1. Turn off the speech processor
2. Hold down the program button while turning the speech processor back on.

Now that I had learned how to do that, my fingers wouldn't leave it alone and I got myself into more trouble! I was glad when bedtime came so I could take it off.

**Saturday, February 17**—Before Myron and I went to Northtown Mall to walk, I checked out Jim Reeves' voice once again. It had recovered and sounded great but it wasn't like I had been hearing it with my Nucleus 22. I wondered, *Which is the real Jim Reeves?*

I had a difficult time understanding the cashiers. I will have to learn how to balance the sensitivity and volume settings. It certainly is not like putting on my Nucleus 22 and turning the sensitivity up or down.

This afternoon Myron, Scott and I went to the airport to pick up my brother, Herb, and his wife, Lila, who had flown in from Yuma. The alarm went off as I went through the security check and I could not understand the security officer. Myron said I was talking loud. Probably some of that was due to nervousness. The security officer did let me go through without any problem. We went and had coffee while we waited for the plane to come in. It was not a pleasant time. The background sounds drowned out Myron's and Scott's voices. I set the sensitivity at Four and that was better. I left it there on the ride home. Nothing was said about my new implant until we got home.

Then, Lila remembered and asked, "How are you doing?" I didn't have time to answer her. She smiled and answered herself.

She said, "It is apparent that you are doing OK!" I was able to follow the four-way conversation quite easily.

Some things that I had not heard before:

1. Our humidifier
2. The freezer of our refrigerator when the door was open
3. Dish washer—It is quiet
4. Lyrics of some songs that I could not understand

**Sunday, February 18**—Myron and I went to church today. The organist was playing softly when we walked into the nave. I thought, *Oh, good. It isn't going to be loud like it was the first Sunday I went to church after my Nucleus 22 was activated.* But I was mistaken. Not only was it loud at the first hymn but it sounded like it had a tummy ache. The singing of the congregation was drowned out. I was able to follow along with the liturgy and I did catch words and phrases during Pastor Strawn's sermon but only if I paid close attention. It was very difficult to chat with my friends out in the narthex after service and I wasn't about to find out if I could hear at Bible study. I opted to go out to breakfast instead.

Myron and I went to Northtown Shopping Center to walk in the mall this afternoon. I chatted with some friends. They surprised me when they said that I seemed to have more confidence. I thought, *Hey, I had confidence with my Nucleus 22!*

We were invited out to Dave's home for dinner this evening. On the way out, I listened to the radio. At times, I understood speech well and other times, I didn't. Music is not as good as it was with my Nucleus 22. I was able to understand the conversation around the dinner table quite well.

**Monday, February 19**—The weather warmed up so I decided to walk to McDonald's this morning. When I stepped outside, I was serenaded by a choir of birds. We have several huge evergreens in our front yard and the birds had chosen those trees to hold a concert. I heard so many different notes and stood in our driveway and listened for several minutes.

The cars and trucks that passed by as I walked were plenty loud but, like Jim Reeves' voice, the sound was not like it had been with my Nucleus 22. Now, the sound was higher pitched than it was with my Nucleus 22. I think the sound with my Nucleus 22 is closer to how someone with normal hearing hears them. I also noticed that I can hear the cars come from a farther distance behind me now.

I found all my friends sitting drinking coffee when I walked into the restaurant. When I sat down, they all gathered round me while I showed them my new toy. A 76-year-old man, who is extremely hearing impaired, was especially interested. He may go for an evaluation.

I called Myron when I got home. I just put the receiver up to my microphone and I was able to hear him quite well. But I wasn't confident enough to pick up the phone when it rang later in the afternoon. I will wait until I get my telephone adapter hooked up before I do that. Anyway, I want to save something for later.

Tuesday, February 20—I had a mapping today. My appointment wasn't until 2:30 but I went in early so I could hear different sounds other than those I hear at home. I also wanted to visit my friend, JoAnn, who had implant surgery on Monday. She was very tired so I did not stay long. Her husband was going to have coffee in the hospital cafeteria so I joined him.

As we sat talking, I was aware of a steady ticking sound. I asked him if he could hear it and he said, "No." I told him it sounded like a clock ticking but I could not see a clock anywhere. When he left, I began to investigate. I didn't have to look long as there was a clock on the wall right behind the table where we were sitting.

I wasn't sure, though, if that was what I heard so I went and checked out two other clocks that were in the room. Both were quiet. There was a doctor sitting near the clock in question so I asked him if he could hear it. He said, "Yes, it is a noisy one!"

When I was sitting in the waiting room of the Cochlear Implant Clinic, I could understand the audiologists as they greeted their patients, "Hi, how are you?" "I'm fine, and you?" A little boy impatiently asked his mother, "What's taking so long?"

Then it was my turn. My MAP had changed some since Thursday and much to my dismay, another electrode made my eye twitch and was deactivated. After mapping, I was sent out into the reception room to see what the real world sounded like. I heard a high-pitched, wailing sound. When I went back in the booth, I was given three more programs. Number Two would take out the high pitches, Number Three, the low pitches and Number Four would give me more volume. I changed to program Number Two before I left for home. I heard wailing on all the other programs.

This evening I listened to *24 Hours*. I heard the speakers very well without using my closed captioning. They were discussing the false labeling that is on a package of cigarettes.

Wednesday, February 21—Myron and I went to our grandson Jeffery's basketball game in the gym of a neighborhood school tonight. The noise was so bad that I could not carry on a conversation with Jeffery's mom and dad. The basketball bouncing and sneakers sliding on the floors sounded like ice cracking or a giant newspaper being crumpled up. I tried to adjust the settings but it didn't help. When we got home, I watched the University of Minnesota Golden Gophers' basketball game. The sound the ball and shoes made sounded the same as it did at Jeffery's game.

Thursday, February 22—I had a scare this morning. When I turned on my processor, I couldn't hear. Just as I was about to begin the troubleshooting, I found the transmitter magnet dangling on the side of my head. Things are getting back to normal for me.

It was warm enough to walk this morning. It was noisy at McDonald's so I fiddled with the controls again. I set the sensitivity on automatic and the volume on Number Nine. I really don't know what I am doing but the music sounded clearer. My friends had left so I don't know how their voices sounded.

When I returned home, there was a message on my answering machine. I couldn't understand more than bits and pieces so I called Myron at work and played it for him. I received another from *Focus News*, our local newspaper. I waited for Myron to come home to tell me what that was about. They want to send a reporter over to interview me for a story about the cochlear implant. I will call them tomorrow.

This evening, Myron and I went to our grandson Jacob's school musical, "A Book is a Magic Carpet." It was in the auditorium at Centennial High School. Can you imagine the noise generated by 100 first graders, their parents, brothers, sisters and grandparents? I was completely comfortable. In fact, I was able to hear the conversation of two men who were sitting behind me. The quality of the sound of the music was great and I was able to understand some of the children's speaking parts. The laughter and applause of the audience sounded like they should sound. Out in the parking lot, I could hear voices. I heard one man clearly say, "How long are you going to be gone?"

Friday, February 23—I had a new mapping today. There were some changes but no more electrodes had to be deactivated. A program to make music sound better was put in one slot. There was a wailing sound as soon as I stepped into the reception room. I was told it is background sounds my brain had not interpreted. I had lunch in the Outside Inn Restaurant. Footsteps, crinkling of newspapers, the cash register opening and closing, and coughing all sound normal. The hospital carts aren't as loud as they were on Tuesday.

Myron and I went out for dinner. I heard the wailing again but I also heard other sounds. One was a scraping sound followed by fast tapping that sounded like metal on metal. I looked around and discovered it was the cook chopping up potatoes and meat on the grill and then scraping the utensils clean.

When we got home, I tried out the music program. I didn't expect any huge improvement as music was already sounding good. I was fooled. I started out once again listening to Jim Reeves. His voice sounded the best ever. It was a mix of my Nucleus 22 and my Nucleus 24 Contour. I listened to other CDs and I was amazed how easy it was to understand the lyrics. I stayed up until 11 o'clock listening to them. It was the longest I have stayed up in a long time.

Saturday, February 24—Myron and I went to our son Dave's alumni basketball game this morning. It was comfortable and it wasn't until after the game was over that I realized the bouncing of the ball did not sound like ice breaking. We stopped at McDonald's for lunch after the game. It was cold in the big room so we went into the playroom. There weren't any kids there so I was able to hear a sound I had not heard in there before—the furnace kicking in.

Tuesday, February 27—Pamela Young, a reporter from *Focus News,* came over to interview me this afternoon. This was the first interview I have had for a newspaper article. My story has been in other publications but I had submitted those. It was a fun hour spent chatting as she took notes. She said the article will appear in a couple of weeks.

**Saturday, March 3**—The wailing sound is gone. I guess my brain has figured out what all the sounds are as I am hearing more things than I did with my Nucleus 22. Once again, I was amazed at the singing of the birds when I stepped outside at seven this morning. I just stood and listened. Every so often I could hear a crow in the distance. It wasn't barking this morning. It sounded like a crow should sound, "caw-caw-caw." I heard a loud rumbling and first thought it was an airplane. Then, I thought it was the traffic on the busy highway nearby. But that was unusual for so early on a Saturday morning. When I heard the train whistle, I knew what was making that loud rumble. It was the train cars rolling down the track.

We went to our grandson Jacob's hockey game this afternoon. It was so noisy in the entryway to the arena that it was impossible to understand my family. I could hear the voices of the people who stood behind me very clearly. At times like this, I yearn for my Nucleus 22. That was much simpler to adjust. All I could think about was, *Why is it so difficult to hear in noise?* Nothing I did with the controls helped. When I sat down, I began to think about what I had been doing. Sometimes it takes a long time for something like this to sink in and this is the ultimate proof. Instead of turning the sensitivity setting down, I was turning the volume down. Once again, when I got home, I took out my user manual and read. It was clear to me, then, what I had been doing wrong.

### Adjusting the Listening Controls

The speech processor features both a microphone and a volume control.

*The microphone sensitivity controls the softest level of sound picked up by the microphone.

Reduce the sensitivity to filter out background noises.

Increase the sensitivity in quiet environments to hear soft sounds.
*The volume controls your perception of loudness.

Reduce the volume if loud sounds are uncomfortably loud.

Increase the volume if speech, including your own voice, is too soft.

Sunday, March 4—I was able to test it today at the Mall of America. When we walked in, it was very loud. I calmly turned the sensitivity down to Number Four. I left the volume setting on Number Four. What a relief! The background noise went down and I was able to hear and understand my family. We had lunch around a long table in a busy restaurant. The waitress stood at the opposite end of the table and I was able to place my order easily. Best of all, I was able to take part in my family's conversation.

After lunch, we went to Camp Snoopy. YIKES! There was a live rock band set up at the entrance. It was loud! I turned both sensitivity and volume down to Number Two but there was no relief. As I stood listening, I observed the other shoppers. Some were keeping time to the music. It was apparent that they were enjoying it. I wasn't! I went back into the mall and set my processor settings back on Number Four. Sounds went back to normal.

Wednesday, March 7—I had another mapping today and received three ACE programs, each at a different speed. Slot one held ACE 14,400 pulses per second; slot two held SPEAK; slot three held

ACE 900 pulses per second; and slot four held ACE 2400 pulses per second. Everything sounds like gushing water with the two fastest ACE speeds. When I went into the cafeteria, I switched to ACE 900, set the sensitivity on Number Four, the volume on Number Five and the water gushing stopped.

**Sunday, March 11**—Went to church this morning. I have lowered both sensitivity and volume settings to Number Three. It is still difficult to understand my friends in the narthex. Women's voices are still too high pitched. The organ sounded very good today but the congregation sings poorly. The women outsing the men.

I heard the train whistle from inside our house. I am understanding more and more on TV without using closed captioning. I can use the telephone with ease. My voice sounds so natural. A battery lasts for about seven hours. I have noticed that when I don't hear something clearly, I strain to the right. I miss my Nucleus 22.

Myron was listening to a CD this evening. He asked, "What does that sound like?"

I said, "It sounds like rushing water."

He said, "It is! " He was listening to a nature CD. It was a waterfall!

**Monday, March 12**—I had my first research session using my Nucleus 24 Contour today. I had speech testing and did quite well. I heard and understood the word "heard" for the first time in four years and "head" sounded like "head" and "had" sounded like "had."

**Wednesday, March 14**—I spent the afternoon shopping at Rosedale Mall today. All went very well. Maybe I will learn to like ACE after all. Women's voices still are too high pitched but I could live with that. I don't remember what SPEAK sounds like anymore. It sure is confusing.

When I heard a telephone ring, it sounded like a telephone should sound. Come to think of it, it didn't sound like we were driving in water on the way to the mall. It is getting more difficult to watch TV with closed captioning as the captioning moves slower than the actual speech. Using the telephone with the adapter is just fine but I suppose I should practice using just the microphone.

I received an invitation to do a presentation for the La Crescent (Minnesota) Lion Club's "Night of Lions" which will be held March 22. It is a community open house concept in an effort to recruit new members. I will also be interviewed by a reporter from the Houston County News, the local newspaper.

Thursday, March 15—The article "Second cochlear implant gives gift of sound to Spring Lake Park resident" appeared today in Focus News, our local newspaper.

Here are two excerpts from the article written by Pamela Young.

Weber said in her book that she is neither a theologian nor a doctor, so she wouldn't delve too deeply into the "How's" and "Why's" of getting back her hearing. As near as she can guess, it was a merging of the right time in her life, personally, and the right time in the development of the technology. Regardless, she does think it is a miracle.

Her second cochlear implant was performed in January 2001, and Weber is still adjusting to the new implant, one that is more technologically advanced than the first. Soon, she will wear the devices for both implants at the same time, allowing her to hear "In Concert" for the first time.

Five months would pass before I heard "In Concert."

# Premonition

*My Journal*

**W**ednesday, March 21—When I was at research today, the side of my head, where my Nucleus 22 receiver is implanted, felt heavy.

**Thursday, March 22**—This morning when I woke up the heaviness was gone. I brushed it off. I thought it was just one more strange hearing phenomenon that had occurred throughout my journey out of silence.

Myron and I went to La Crescent, Minnesota where I gave a presentation at "Night of Lions." It was a three hour drive along the Mississippi River. While we drove, we listened to songs from the 1950s and 1960s and watched bald eagles gliding over the water in search of their breakfast. We also saw many perched high in the trees enjoying their morning catch. We stopped several times to try to hear them but they were too engrossed in eating and kept quiet.

When we reached La Crescent, we checked into the motel and went to the Commodore Club Restaurant to meet the Lions Club President for dinner. It was then on to the community center. It was quiet when we walked in but as more and more people streamed in, it got very noisy. I was happy to follow John Prinzler, of the *Houston County News,* into a private room for my interview.

As usual, when I start talking about my cochlear implant, I got carried away and we lost track of time. Someone had to come to remind us that I had a job to do. When we got into the meeting room, it was time for my presentation. I wasn't ready to start talking again. I just could not get into a natural flow and I relied heavily on my notes. Even then, I made mistakes. It did help to recall what a sister-in-law had once told me, "The speaker knows his topic much better than the audience."

This was one time I hoped the assumption was true. It probably was, or the audience was just being kind, as I did get a nice round of applause when I finished speaking and compliments as we chatted over coffee.

Friday, March 23—We listened to music again on the way home. We hadn't driven far before I noticed my right eye was "tearing." By the time we reached home, the right side of my head felt heavy again and there was pressure in my right ear canal.

Saturday and Sunday, March 24 and 25—I found out that it was not a phenomenon. The symptoms continued all weekend as I watched the NCAA March Madness basketball games and on Saturday evening when my family went to the Pizza Factory.

Monday, March 26—The symptoms continued and I began to wonder if something was wrong with my Nucleus 22 implant.

Tuesday, March 27—The heaviness was still there so I had my doctor check it when I went for my research session. Except for finding the site swollen, he could not find anything wrong. He said I may have an allergy or that my glasses had shifted.

Wednesday, March 28—All was okay. I spent the day at home where it is quiet.

Thursday, March 29—I listened to music while I folded laundry. Within a few minutes, my right eye was again "tearing" and the side of my face began to feel heavy. I took my glasses off and it kept getting worse. I took my processor off and kept both it and my glasses off for two hours.

The symptoms went away. I put my processor back on and kept my glasses off. As soon as I began to listen to music, the symptoms returned. I stopped listening to music and the symptoms went away.

**Friday, Saturday and Sunday, March 30–31, April 1**—The symptoms came and went over the weekend, depending on the environment. Since I had previously experienced the same symptoms, but not to the extent that I am experiencing them now, I'm not too worried.

**Monday, April 2**—I received a copy of the article written by John Prinzler titled "Hearing for the first time in a decade inspires woman to share her story" that appeared in the March 29 issue of the *Houston County News*. Here are some excerpts:

> Weber was asked to speak before the La Crescent Lions by Gale Bruessel, the club's first vice-president. Bruessel said she heard Weber speak at a Lion's mid-winter convention two years ago in Austin, Minnesota. "It brought a tear to my eye when she said she was able to hear the birds for the first time," said Bruessel. "I was touched by her talk and by the fact that the Lions was able to help her."

> She (Weber) said she doesn't take for granted listening to her favorite sounds: birds singing, the voices of her grandchildren, and listening to music, especially country western. Her hearing had been so bad that she was never able to hear the birds."

Although the cochlear implant in her left ear is the only one being utilized now by Weber, she said both implants will be used by her in about three weeks.

She said she needs to get used to using her left one (Nucleus 24 Contour).

"I had both of the implants on for five hours after my left one was activated," she said. "It was beautiful. The sound was very balanced."

Thursday, April 12—I had an appointment for a mapping today. At the close of the appointment, my audiologist surprised me by asking me if I would like to wear my Nucleus 22 for the day. She knew I was going to be at the clinic that evening for a presentation by an Advanced Bionics representative. She said I could leave my processor with her at the end of the meeting. It had been three days short of two months since I last heard with it, yet I expected to take off from the day of my Nucleus 24 Contour activation. I was very disappointed. My Nucleus 22 did not cooperate.

Another patient was scheduled so I was told to wait in the reception room while she went to get my processor. My friend Emil, who also has a cochlear implant, was waiting for his appointment. I sat down to chat with him. Just as I turned my processor on, Emil laughed. I could have cried! The sound was so sharp it made my teeth sting. I turned the sensitivity down to Number One. It was no longer as loud but the sound was very clickety and full of static. I thought, *Boy, I sure can use a mapping!*

I had lunch at the Outside Inn Restaurant. I definitely experienced surround sound and I could tell the direction where sounds were coming from. The noise in the restaurant wasn't as bothersome as it is with only my Nucleus 24 Contour.

Myron picked me up at noon and I went to Rosedale Mall. On the drive over, I understood much of what was said on the radio as well as understanding Myron over the sounds of the road.

The first thing I did when I got to the mall was to hold the transmitter-magnet away from my head. No way could I get along only with my Nucleus 22. Then, I did the same thing with the magnet of my Nucleus 22. The sounds were better with my Nucleus 24 Contour but, together, there certainly was surround sound. Each added dimension to the other. Everything had a normal sound. There was no reverberation. Even using the speech strategy, ACE, on my Nucleus 24 Contour, and SPEAK on my Nucleus 22, the sounds were processed at the same time. The only thing that seemed strange was that when I placed my order at Arby's Restaurant, I heard my voice on both sides. It was so much more pleasant strolling through the mall.

When the batteries of my Nucleus 24 Contour went dead, I experienced something very surprising. I could still hear! When I changed the batteries, I heard the click and the grinding sound the battery door made as I slid it open. I heard the clunk as I laid the batteries on the table and the rattle of the new batteries as I took them out of the plastic bag. Then, I heard the clunk as I put the newly charged batteries in the battery case and the click as I slid the battery compartment door shut.

I heard the Advanced Bionics representative very well this evening. The right side (Nucleus 22) seemed to be favored but when I held the transmitter-magnet of my Nucleus 24 Contour away from my head, the volume went down. When I did the same with my Nucleus 24 Contour, the volume was louder than with my Nucleus 22. With both on, the sound was very, very full. The processors kept time with each other but I did hear his voice on each side. My Nucleus 24 Contour side sounded like I was listening to a radio. The Nucleus 22 side sounded the way I was hearing him in person.

Once again, I found it difficult to part with my Nucleus 22 at the close of the evening. I would have liked to have continued using both processors but there was more listening to do with my Nucleus 24 Contour.

I had a nice surprise toward the end of April. I received an invitation to give a presentation at the National Cochlear Implant Association, Inc. (CIAI) Convention that will be held at the Marriott City Center in downtown Minneapolis on July 13-16. I could not turn down such a great opportunity to share my story. I will also be showing the video of my Nucleus 24 Contour activation.

I am a bit nervous as this will be the largest group I have spoken to and there will be many there who also have implants. Certainly, there will be many in the audience who know more about the cochlear implant than I do. I also feel sad as the convention is on the same weekend as my 45th class reunion. I will not be able to show off my wonderful hearing to my classmates.

Thursday, April 13-Wednesday, May 23—I spent the time experimenting with SPEAK and ACE at speeds of 14,400 pulses per second, 2400 pulses per second and 900 pulses per second. Sounds using 14,400 pulses per second were high pitched and everything sounded like water bubbling. I experienced tinnitus on the second day. On the fifth day, I switched to the SPEAK strategy. There was a high pitched wailing sound and voices had a nasal sound. The tinnitus returned on the third day.

It took awhile to get used to using ACE at 2400 pulses per second.

I heard low-pitched sounds I thought were processor sounds until I realized they were actual environment sounds such as the hum of traffic on the freeway. High pitches and low pitches seem to be blended. The birds sing beautifully—from the high pitched twitter of the wrens to the cooing of the doves. Telephone, television and music all sound good.

Everything sounds much the same using ACE at 900 pulses per second as it is using ACE 2400 pulses per second. An added perk is that I get five more hours of battery life. I gave SPEAK one more try and it no longer sounds good. I think ACE 900 is the strategy that is best for me.

# Missing Puzzle Pieces Found

When I had finished trying ACE at the three different speeds, 900 pulses per second, 2400 pulses per second, and 14,400 pulses per second, I thought all my experimenting was finished and I would be given the strategy I liked best. I was wrong.

Along with giving ACE and SPEAK one more trial run, I had to give CIS a fair chance. I tried each strategy sequentially for two weeks. Then, to determine which strategy I performed best with, I underwent speech recognition testing in the Clinical Psychoacoustics Laboratory. The results of the speech recognition tests helped me choose the strategy that was the best for me and I began to use it full-time.

*My Journal with SPEAK*

**Wednesday, May 23**—The volume Myron has the car radio set at was loud with my sensitivity set on Number Six and volume at Number Seven so I turned the sensitivity down to Number Three and volume down to Number Four.

Music is loud at McDonald's but I can't tell if the person singing is a man or a woman. All voices have a nasal or foghorn sound and I hear lots of squeaking. I understand voices but I don't like the sound. I hope it changes.

**Thursday, May 24**—I turned both sensitivity and volume down to Number Three. TV is loud but Myron says it is not loud at all.

Things did change during the day yesterday. Music sounded good in the afternoon and I understood quite a lot on TV. It amazes me how these changes happen. I was feeling so down when I went to bed last night and I hated to put my processor on this morning. Telephone is fine. Myron is getting confused. One day, I can understand him and the next day, I can't. Birds sound beautiful. Voices still have the nasal sound. There is no tinnitus.

Friday, May 25—Things are even louder today but I kept settings at Number Three. When I stepped outside to bring the morning paper in, I stood and listened to the singing of the birds. I could also hear the hum of the traffic on the highway. My batteries last about 22 hours. I turned both settings up to Number Four later in the day.

Saturday, May 26—The high-pitched squeal I heard at my activation is back. Speech can improve but I could learn to live with it the way it is. Myron and I drove to his hometown, Chaska, Minnesota, this afternoon. We drove out to the country to see the farm where he grew up. All the while, he talked about growing up. We retraced the bus route he took every morning and evening to and from school. It was pretty wonderful to be able to chat like that.

Sunday, May 27—Speech is very unclear—maybe I need new batteries.

Monday, May 28—Speech is still nasal sounding.

Tuesday, May 29—I turned my processor on automatic loudness. Still no tinnitus.

Wednesday, May 30—Speech is still nasal sounding. I have it set on Number Four. I had problems hearing in the waiting room of the Cochlear Implant Clinic so I turned the settings up to Number Seven. I could hear better but the background noise is irritating.

**Thursday, May 31**—Sensitivity and volume set on Number Six is too loud for environmental sounds but okay for speech.

**Friday, June 1**—I went out for breakfast with the neighbor gals. I needed some help placing my order but I was able to keep up with the conversation quite well. My brother, Herb, and his wife, Lila, came to spend the weekend with us. Our sons' families dropped over to visit with them. Conversing wasn't perfect but was okay.

**Saturday, June 2**—We went to Perkins' Restaurant for breakfast. Our table was smack dab in the middle of the dining room. It was very noisy as I could hear the people all around me. It was very difficult conversing at our table. Myron and I went to our grand-daughter Chelsea's gymnastic recital in the evening. The music sounded very good. We all went to Pizza Hut after the recital and it was easy to converse.

**Sunday, June 3**—We went to church this morning. We sat up closer to the front. I heard the sermon quite well. The car radio was loud and there is still a nasal sound to speech. I am getting used to it.

**Monday, June 4**—I put new batteries in my processor and they lasted for 32 hours.

**Tuesday, June 5**—Last day of SPEAK. I could get along with this strategy but I feel I can do better. As I did with my Nucleus 22, I feel like something is missing and that it is just within reach. One thing I am thankful for is that I have not experienced any more tinnitus. I switched to ACE at 6:30 this evening. Everything sounded scratchy and high pitched for the first few minutes and then began to smooth out. My processor is set at sensitivity Number Eight and volume is at Number Seven. When the Minnesota Twins came on, I turned the sound off and listened to my CDs. They sounded okay right away but the more I listened, the better they sounded. I understood Myron without difficulty. I am amazed that something can sound so bad and then, in a short time, begin to sound great. I have been through the process countless times but it still amazes me.

## With ACE-Advanced Combination Encoders

**Wednesday, June 6**—I turned the sensitivity and volume down to Number Six but when I turned TV on, the fellow who was speaking sounded so squeaky, I turned them back to Number Seven. That got rid of the squeaks. On the ride over to McDonald's, I could understand quite a lot on the radio. Music sounded fine. The road noise wasn't so loud. Here at McDonald's, the music is okay (if you like that type). A woman's voice is squeaky but the instruments sound fine. I can hear the hash brown fryer's "beep, beep, beeps" but they sound more squeaky than they did with SPEAK.

Last night I woke up hearing little squeaks in my left ear, the Nucleus 24 Contour side, and there was mild tinnitus across the top of my head. Both were gone this morning. The right side of my face felt heavy and tight again but it didn't last long.

I heard the Wednesday 1 p.m. tornado test siren while I was watching TV even with the door shut. Voices on the answering machine sounded muffled. Myron and I went to our grandson Jeffery's baseball game. It was comfortable. I could understand the comments of parents who were sitting behind me.

**Thursday, June 7**—TV was loud when I put my processor on so I turned the settings to Number Six. Myron sounded like he was talking with his mouth full of food. The sounds of traffic were okay on my morning walk. The hash brown fryer beeps aren't squeaky this morning. I can understand lots of what the fellows who are sitting behind me are talking about. They are talking about some place where parking is not permitted and they said it makes no sense! The sounds of newspapers aren't so loud and squeaky today.

**Friday, June 8**—Things are changing rapidly. Speech is much better. The nasal sound is gone and Myron's voice sounds so much better. It was easy conversing over coffee with my neighbor, Barb, this morning. Birds are singing beautifully. Music sounds great and I understood much of TV without closed captioning. We went to our city parade last night and the bagpipes sounded like I remember from years ago. Last year, they screeched. The bands sounded wonderful. There seems to be a better blending of low and high pitches and nothing seems to be unusually loud or soft.

**Saturday, June 9**—The birds sang so pretty on my walk this morning. I am hearing different ones than those I already hear. It began to rain while I was on my walk and the sound of the raindrops on my umbrella was so soothing. I didn't notice the sound of traffic so it must be much less harsh.

Myron and I took our grandkids, Brandon, 3, and Ashley, 2, to Como Zoo this afternoon. I was able to understand both very well. As we were walking, I could hear a lion roar in the distance. It took quite a while before we saw him. Not only did we see him but his entire family. Mother was laying in the shade resting and her cubs were playing. They were running and jumping on her. It is amazing how much patience she had.

Sunday, June 10—I woke up with a stiff neck and a headache this morning so I didn't go to church. I doubt that it is related to my implant.

Monday, June 11—I understood my friends at McDonald's this morning. The beeps of the hash brown machine are now loud and clear. We were under a tornado watch this evening. I could hear a siren way off in the distance while I was in the house watching TV. I have been turning sensitivity up to Number Eight while watching TV. I listened to tapes of songs from the 1950s and was thrilled to be able to understand the lyrics that had always evaded me. Some songs were "Purple People Eater," "Chattanooga Shoeshine Boy," "Green Door," "The Thing," and "Oh, My Papa."

Tuesday, June 12—I heard the announcer well on the car radio this morning. He was talking about the need to have a license to play golf in England. I understood the fellows sitting in the booth behind me at McDonald's; I try not to but it is hard. I feel like I am a spy.

Wednesday, June 13—I went to the dentist this morning. It is fun because everyone is so excited that I can hear now. My dentist is the kindest, most understanding young man in the world. When I first began seeing him, I was totally deaf and he took the time to write down everything he was going to do. Now I can understand him through his mask. It's fun to be able to hear him and his assistant chat while he works. And, of course, it is even nice to hear the sound of the drill instead of just feeling the vibrations.

I took a walk in the rain this afternoon just so I could hear the drops fall on my umbrella. I called Myron without the use of my telephone adapter. I heard him well but I prefer using the adapter as I have to hold the receiver so tight up against my microphone.

**Thursday, June 14**—I went to Rosedale Mall this afternoon and then to the clinic for a Cochlear Implant Board meeting to discuss plans for the welcoming committee at the CIAI convention in July. We will wear red T-shirts to make us stand out from the other convention attendees.

**Friday, June 15**—Myron and I went over to our son Ken's home to set up a tent and tables for our 40th anniversary celebration. It has been a very cold and rainy spring and today was no exception. Ken had just built a beautiful wood patio outside the sliding glass door to their basement family room. We were talking about it being a great dance floor. Our grandson piped up, "Grandma, you have to dance with your husband." I love to be able to hear those funny things my grandchildren say.

**Saturday, June 16**—Put to the test, our big day. I woke up to a bright day. I looked outside and the sun was shining brightly. There wasn't a cloud in the sky. There were about 100 guests in attendance. Both old and new friends came to celebrate with us. All knew I had been deaf and that now I could hear with my cochlear implant but many had not witnessed it. They were thrilled.

The party was outside. The kids had done a terrific job decorating the garage and with the refreshments. Our cake had a picture of our wedding day on the frosting. It was difficult talking to my friends in the garage but outside, it was no problem. I had a hard time regulating the settings so I finally just set both on Number Five and left them there. I did what Jacob said. I danced with my wonderful husband. The picture adorns the cover of this book.

**Sunday, June 17**—As a "thank you" to our kids, we took them out for pizza today. The clouds came back and it began to rain again. It was a bit difficult to follow the conversation. I set the sensitivity on Number Four and volume on Number Seven. I didn't have a chance to tell if it helped as we left soon after.

Monday, June 18—We drove in a downpour to the clinic for my research session. I can't imagine not hearing the rain slap against the windshield. I could hear the radio announcer over the din. He was telling about storm warnings.

When I am in the Outside Inn Restaurant, I have my settings on Number Two for sensitivity and Number Five for volume. I am learning! When I am at the clinic, I turn the sensitivity to Number Seven and volume to Number Five. All is comfortable.

Tuesday, June 19—All is well! This is the last day on ACE. I could easily continue with this strategy as everything sounds so natural.

*With CIS—Continuous Interleaved Sampling*

Wednesday, June 20—There wasn't a noticeable change when I switched over to CIS. Sounds are maybe a bit mellower. Music does not sound as good as it did with ACE. I can understand Myron when he speaks to me.

Thursday, June 21—Myron's voice now sounds as though he is gargling. The car radio is okay. Music sounds okay. It was much more difficult to understand my friends at McDonald's but they are understanding as they know what is going on. Music is not as good. Jim Reeves' voice is different again. Birds continue to sound beautiful.

Friday, June 22—Things sounded loud when I put my processor on this morning. Sensitivity was set on Number Five and volume on Number Eight.

I changed to Five and Six and it sounded better. Myron's voice still sounds like gargling. Music and TV are okay once I get the settings adjusted.

**Saturday, June 23**—Things seem to sound the best if I have sensitivity on Eight and then adjust the volume until it sounds good. I haven't experienced any tinnitus. Our grandson slept over last night and we went out to dinner at Timber Lodge. I heard him well. I had the sensitivity set at Number Four.

**Sunday, June 24**—I went to a 50th wedding anniversary celebration at our church this afternoon. The commons room has always been a challenge to hear in as the acoustics are very bad. Again, I set sensitivity on Number Four and volume on Number Six. I got along okay except voices sounded muffled.

**Monday, June 25**—Had a quiet day at home alone. I watched the Minnesota Twins baseball game.

**Tuesday, June 26**—Voices are still muffled but environmental sounds are fine.

**Wednesday, June 27**—I figured out what voices sound like. People sound like they are talking with their mouths full of food. Sounds mushy. People on TV do, too. Nothing has changed since the first day I began to use CIS. I know now what "I hear but don't understand" means. Myron keeps asking me, "How many more days with this thing?"

**Thursday, June 28**—Voices still sound "mushy" but environmental sounds are fine. I have a constant headache but, thankfully, no tinnitus. I wouldn't want to be on this strategy if I had something special to do. Myron has to repeat everything several times before I understand him. Women's voices are a bit easier to understand.

**Friday–Sunday, June 29-July 1**—Voices have not improved. We went to Osakis to visit my sister on Sunday. I did not enjoy listening to my CDs on the drive. My sister, Ellie, also has the Nucleus 22 cochlear implant and is doing well. We spent the day in the beautiful city park.

**Monday, July 2**—Elevators sound bubbly instead of rattly and they give me a headache. I spoke with a cochlear implant candidate and his wife in the clinic today. It was very difficult to understand them. Quite likely, they didn't think I was doing very well with my implant. I hope I didn't dissuade him from having the implant. If I didn't know there was something better for me, I would be satisfied to hear the way I do but I am glad I am almost finished with this strategy.

**Tuesday, July 3**—Had my final testing with the three strategies and it is no surprise that I did the best with ACE. That will be the strategy I will be using full time. I switched to ACE right after my testing and it was like my head had cleared up after having a bad head cold. The voices I heard in the clinic were clear again and Myron's voice, that had been the worst of all, was again easy to understand.

On the drive home, I listened to the radio and it took a while before I realized I could hear much of what was said. I understood most of what the news reporters talked about on world news and later as I watched the Twins game. I heard the announcers very well. I listened to some tapes on my boom box and Patti Page sang "Tennessee Waltz" and "Mockingbird Hill" very well.

I do believe I have mastered my Nucleus 24 Contour and that I have found the missing puzzle pieces. I am now ready to meet the challenge of bilateral hearing.

# Final Stretch

*My Journal*

**Wednesday, July 4**—I got up early today. As I was dressing, I heard the train whistle. On my morning walk, the birds sang even more beautifully. The doves, that I had missed so much, were again cooing. I found my friend, Bruce, at McDonald's. He speaks so fast and I always had a difficult time understanding him. Today, I didn't have any problems. The rock music sounded clear but again, I didn't like that type. I have my sensitivity set on Number Five and volume on Number Six. The traffic sounds might have been too loud. I will have to see about that. The hash brown machine beeps sounded like they should.

This afternoon, we drove to Buffalo, Minnesota for a barbeque at our son Dave's house. As we were driving through St. Michaels, Myron rolled the car windows down. I knew why immediately. The church bells were tolling. He parked along the street until they had finished ringing. It sounded so beautiful! That was one sound I had not had the opportunity to enjoy even with my Nucleus 22. I heard the tornado test siren and the train whistle when I was outdoors playing with our grandchildren, Brandon and Ashley.

**Thursday, July 5**—It is so nice to put my processor on in the morning and know I will understand Myron better. He is much happier! Everything sounds so natural. I heard a helicopter off in the distance long before I saw it.

**Friday, July 6**—When I put my processor on this morning, I could hear the hair dryer from around the corner of the kitchen as Myron dried his hair. I have both the sensitivity and volume set on Number Five except when I watch TV. Then, I turn my sensitivity up to Number Seven. I understand so much more on TV without closed captioning. Music sounds wonderful.

Saturday–Tuesday, July 7–10—All is well! I can understand the answering machine so much better now and I use the telephone with ease. All birds sing beautifully and human voices no longer have a nasal sound.

Wednesday, July 11—Everything sounds wonderful. I continue to pick up lyrics of songs that I had not understood before.

Thursday, July 12—I spent the day practicing for my Sunday presentation at the Cochlear Implant Association, Inc. (CIAI) convention. I am nervous.

Friday–Sunday, July 13–15—Today was the first day of the convention. It was pretty exciting when I registered and was given my name badge with a ribbon attached indicating that I was a speaker. It was very noisy in the hotel lobby so I did a lot of adjusting on my processor.

As a member of the welcoming committee, I met many wonderful people. One of the first was a young lady from Canada who had come to the convention seeking information about the cochlear implant. I have to admit I had a difficult time understanding her. I think she did better reading my lips. I began to wonder if I would be able to motivate her to have a cochlear implant. I was happy when my friend, JoAnn, arrived. She is nearer to her age and also prelingual. I introduced them and they spent much time together.

There were so many workshops and socials that it was difficult to choose which ones I wanted to attend. I attended the

CIAI Chapter coordinator meeting and the "First Timers" social and the Welcome Reception on Friday. It was great to visit the exhibits. Of course, I was drawn to the Cochlear Corporation booth where the behind-the-ear processor, called the 3G, was on display. The exhibit drew many admiring teenagers. Although there are many colors to choose from, that is not what appealed to me. What I liked was how small it is and that it does not have a long cable. When I begin wearing my Nucleus 22, I will have two body processors with long cables. This time, I am certain to get a behind-the-ear processor as I had exchanged the ESPrit I had received at my activation. I have a certificate safely tucked away at home waiting for the release of the 3G.

I attended the "What's New for Nucleus 22 and Nucleus 24 Recipients" presented by Christine Writer, M.A., CCC-A of Cochlear Americas. The upcoming Nucleus 24-ESPrit 3G was of particular interest to me. In the evening, I went to the Adult/Teen Banquet.

On Sunday morning, I attended the workshop, "Clinical Study of Bilateral Cochlear Implantation in Adults," presented by Jennifer L. Arcaroli, M.S., CCC-A from Cochlear Corporation. The purpose of the study was to evaluate the advantages of bilateral implantation compared to one implant. Some potential advantages are to hear sounds on both sides of our head, to locate the source of the sound and improved hearing in the midst of noise. The study will also help to determine which is the best side to implant for single implantation.

I was happy to hear the number of those participating in the clinical studies. I am proud of the pioneers and I am proud to be one of them in having a sequential cochlear implant.

My presentation was at 1:30 p.m. The attendees were very slow at arriving but they soon began to trickle in. By the time I stepped up to the podium, all the chairs were filled and some teenagers were sitting in front of me on the floor. I was surprised when I saw Dr. Jon Shallop, Ph.D., Assistant Professor of Audiology at the Mayo Clinic in Rochester, Minnesota. His presence did not make me nervous. It made me proud.

Usually, when I give a presentation, I am pressed for time. Today, I had an hour and a half to tell my story. I shared some of my time with my friend, JoAnn. Part of the time was used up by getting the VCR working so I could show the video of my Nucleus 24 Contour activation. I think my presentation was well received as I received a hearty round of applause when I finished speaking. I also believe the information I shared about the cochlear implant was accurate. No one corrected me.

It was a great three days. I met so many wonderful and helpful people. Rosemary, Carol and Julie have all promised to keep in touch with me. Rosemary has a cousin living in the area and she is spending a week with her before flying home to California. We are going to get together for lunch one day.

**Friday, July 20**—Rosemary came over today and we went out to lunch at Perkins' Restaurant. We were led to a booth that was partly obscured to other patrons. We sat and talked for several hours. Of course, we shared our stories with our waitress.

Rosemary told me I should get an e-mail address so I can subscribe to Cochlear Corporation's Nucleus Forum. All this was foreign to me so I will have to ask my son, Scott, to help me with this.

For now, though, I have something much more exciting on my mind. I have reached another turning point in my journey. On Tuesday, I will have my Nucleus 22 remapped and begin to wear it full-time along with my Nucleus 24 Contour.

# Dream Come True

**Tuesday, July 24**—My Nucleus 22 was remapped today and I began using both implants full time. After almost six months of non-use, my right side is alive again with the wonders of sound. The sounds are not as clear as they were the day my Nucleus 24 Contour was activated. There is a lot of static. I went to show off my new hearing in the research laboratory and when I was there, the doorbell rang. It was the first time in five years I had heard it.

Sounds are processed at the same time but I hear them differently with each processor. The sounds are clear and higher pitched on my Nucleus 24 Contour side. The sounds with my Nucleus 22 are rough around the edges and lower pitched. I understand speech but it was difficult understanding what was said on TV this evening.

**Friday, July 27**—I had coffee with my friend, Barb, in the noisy food court at Northtown Mall today. It was easy to hear and understand her. It was also pleasant chatting as we strolled through the Mall. I am enjoying true stereo now when my CDs are played on my stereo. I hear some musical tones on my left side and some on my right. The birds continue to hide from me but now when I hear them sing, it's easier to find the tree they are perched in. The tree is not always on my left side now. Television is still giving me a problem.

**Saturday, July 28**—Myron and I took our grandkids, Jacob and Chelsea, to the Anoka County Fair today. I heard Chelsea's soft little voice much better. While Grandpa and Uncle Scott took them for rides on the Midway, I went to the Riders of the Purple Sage stage show. Oh, how beautiful was the music. I was even able to understand the names of the songs when they were introduced. I had not been able to do that for many years.

**Sunday, July 29**—Today Myron and I went to the 150th anniversary celebration of his hometown, Chaska, Minnesota. We attended a church service held in a tent. We arrived late so we had to sit in the back. Even then, I heard the sermon clearly.

During the sermon, I heard the loud, shrill song of a strange bird. Myron told me his grandmother called them "hotbirds." I found out later that they really have a name. They are cicadas. Like the grasshopper I had mistaken for a bird, they are not birds. They are large insects called locusts.

After the service, we watched the two-hour parade. The bands sounded great and the bagpipes sounded even better than they had at our city parade. A parade is not a parade without the "pipers."

**Monday, July 30**—I can easily tell when the battery of my Nucleus 24 Contour goes dead but cannot always tell when the one in my Nucleus 22 processor does. The battery of my Nucleus 22 lasts about 16 hours and the battery in my Nucleus 24 Contour lasts about 11 hours.

**Tuesday, July 31**—My Nucleus 22 processor began crackling today so I changed the long cable. The crackling stopped but sounds are still full of static. I have noticed my Nucleus 24 Contour is no longer as dominant. The two are "coming together" nicely. Music sounds great both on my boom box and in stereo. There is still lots of competition with television. Environment sounds are so natural. Speech gets better and better.

**Thursday, August 2**—Things are much the same. Sounds with my Nucleus 22 still have static. I changed the short cable but it did not help. I also tried a new microphone but that was not the answer to my problems. Now I need to have the sensitivity at Number Five if I use it alone. I have an appointment for a mapping soon so I hope a new MAP is the answer.

**Friday–Sunday, August 3–5**—I am experimenting with the settings on each processor. The environment changes so often and I have to do a lot of adjusting with the sensitivity of each processor. I found that I hear the best if I have the volume and sensitivity of my Nucleus 24 Contour set on Number Four and Number Three, respectively. Then I have the sensitivity of my Nucleus 22 set on Number Four. It is amazing how soft the sounds become when the battery of either processor goes dead. Each adds so much dimension to the other. Music continues to sound great and I think I have mastered television.

Since sounds are higher pitched with my Nucleus 24 Contour and lower with my Nucleus 22, I now turn the sensitivity of my Nucleus 22 up a notch. Voices mesh better. I hear so much better when I am in a noisy environment. It is comfortable wearing both processors. I feel balanced. I can now tell which battery goes dead.

My journal entries ended there. I think the reason they ended is that I had more time to write while I was waiting to begin using my Nucleus 22. I had taken a leave of absence from volunteering in Project Read, did not participate in research and had not received any speaking engagements. Now that I had reached my goal of using both processors, I was again ready to get on with my life.

I returned to my little "classroom" in the pediatric clinic to read to the little patients. It was easier to understand the little ones above the noise of those children who chose to play instead of sitting and listening to the story. The choice of stories had not changed during my six-month absence. They still wanted to hear about the adventures of Corduroy and Franklin the Turtle and to join me in singing, "I'll Love You for Always." I would have been content to continue reading indefinitely but my stay was cut short. My long ago dream of becoming a teacher was about to come true.

That fall, when school resumed, our daughter-in-law, Sharon, was appointed to the school board of Prince of Peace Christian Day School and was elected chairperson. Myron soon joined the board and was appointed secretary.

After the first meeting, Sharon stopped in with Myron. They had big plans for Grandma. The school had openings for a pre-school teacher's aide as well as an Olive Tree (Latchkey) morning supervisor. Sharon and Myron thought this was a perfect opportunity for me as they knew I loved children. They didn't think I should apply for just one position. They thought I could handle both. I wasn't sure I could handle even one. The more they talked about it, the more interested I became. I do love children and I also love a challenge. I applied for both positions and was hired. My goal was to make it through one year.

Olive Tree went well the first Monday. There were about six children there. I am terrible at remembering names so I made name tags for each child. The parents were happy to know I would be there every morning and the word spread. Attendance increased and soon I was supervising as many as 20 students from 6:30 a.m. until 8:15 a.m., Monday through Friday.

My time spent in Olive Tree was very interesting. It was quite a diverse group of children from Grades K–8. Believe me, it was a challenge. We played games and made crafts but mostly, I was just a presence in the room, keeping them in line. They broke into groups and did their own thing. Oh, yes, there were some times when they had disagreements and I had to step in and referee. My lack of experience did show in some instances. Those I brought to the attention of the school principal. All in all, things went okay. There were times when the noise became stressful. At those times, I stood in the doorway.

The first day I spent in the pre-kindergarten room wasn't nearly as pleasant. The noise generated by 16 active and happy four- and five-year-olds was a bit too much for me. I gave my notice at the end of the first day. I did agree to continue until a full-time aide was found and then I would be the substitute aide. Several weeks went by before the position was filled. By then, I had learned how to adjust my processors to adapt to the noise and I had become quite attached to the job and the children.

It was mighty loud in the pre-kindergarten classroom but I didn't have time to stand in the doorway. I didn't have great difficulty understanding the children but it helped greatly when the teacher suggested I show and explain my cochlear implant to the children.

*Dora reading to Justine and other Pre-K children.*

Five years ago, after I received my Nucleus 22, I had visited each classroom and told the students about the cochlear implant. The kindergarten class was the most interested so it did not surprise me that the pre-kindergarten students gave me their undivided attention. They got right up by me, pushing each other away with some even trying to climb up onto my lap so they could see better. It did help in later communication. I smile now as I remember a little girl named Justine. Whenever she talked to me, she looked at me and spoke loudly.

I was kept busy helping with crafts, supervising at recess time and at snack time, keeping the little ones occupied and happy, teaching them to share and get along with each other. Their teacher was in the room to handle any problems that arose. My grandson, Justin, who was in the class, posed my biggest challenge. He had to learn to share Grandma. By the time a full-time

*Dora explaining to the inquisitive little Pre-K children how she can hear with her cochlear implant.*

*Writing a book is not an easy task.*

aide was found, Justin had made friends and was willing to share me with them. It didn't take long to become quite attached to the little ones. Luckily for me, I got to return to the classroom quite often as a substitute.

I had completed the Nucleus 24 Contour research projects and I could not resume research with my Nucleus 22 until my hearing had stabilized. I was not volunteering in Project Read and had my afternoons free. Then, I began to think about learning how to use our computer. We had owned one for several years but like anything technical, it frightened me so Myron was the sole user. The closest I got to it was the chair I placed next to Myron as I dictated my speeches to him. It wasn't until after Christmas and after several long distance calls made to and received from Rosemary in California that I got up the courage to at least try to learn.

Luckily, my son, Scott, is a computer designer. He came over to help me. He found a provider for me and the next thing I knew, I had my own e-mail address. One problem remained. I did not know how to type.

I had tried typing in high school but I only attended one class. I could not hear my teacher when she gave us instructions. I did take typing classes in adult education after I graduated but I did not finish that course either. However, I did retain something from those classes. I remembered the proper way to place my fingers on the keys but for the first few days, I just pecked away with one finger.

The first e-mail I sent was, of course, to Rosemary. It did take a mighty long time to peck out the message but when it was finished, it made me proud. With her encouragement, I kept at it and soon I was typing by using the fingers of both hands—very slowly, but I was typing. I became so efficient that I began to e-mail my bionic humor message to the editor of our cochlear implant club newsletter.

I didn't have many addresses in my address book and I wanted more so I looked at the information that Rosemary had given me about the Cochlear Americas Nucleus Forum. I subscribed and the next day, I received a Forum Digest. I just read the posts for several days before jumping in. It took a while for me to become an established poster. I think what broke the ice and made me feel a part of the group was a post I wrote that was quite embarrassing. But I rose to the challenge and with the use of humor, I redeemed myself.

A thread on mastoidectomies was then going on the Forum. In a post I sent, I inadvertently typed mastectomy. That caught the attention of many and I received a lot of teasing. I didn't know how else to respond except to say that I knew better; I had just made a silly error. Then, I remembered an experience I had the previous summer.

Myron and I had taken a vacation in Iowa and toured the research laboratories where my family's otosclerosis genetic linkage study is taking place. We had stayed at a motel the night before. Being an early riser, I was down in the lobby drinking coffee at 6 a.m. Usually, I have the lobby to myself but this time was different. Soon, all the tables were occupied.

I noticed a family at the other end of the room. The son and daughter were sitting on the stairway and the mom and dad were standing. There was an extra chair by my table so I asked the mom if she would like to join me. She accepted my invitation and soon we were talking away.

When she asked me where we were going and I told her we were going to the University of Iowa, she got excited. They were from Spokane and were there to bring their daughter to the University of Iowa where she was to resume her studies in audiology. That got me excited!

I told her about my cochlear implants. That made her even more excited! She shouted across the room to her daughter, "Hey, Kristine, come over here. This lady has those implants!"

You better believe that all eyes in the room were on me and they were not focused on my ears! When Kristine joined us, I calmly reached in my shirt pocket, pulled out my Nucleus 22 processor and, with people looking on, I told her all about the cochlear implant.

I have kept in touch with Kristine's mother since that meeting and she has kept me up-to-date with Kristine's career as an audiologist. After graduating from the University of Iowa, she accepted a job in New Castle, Delaware. She recently passed her state audiology exams and is now a licensed audiologist.

That post did lighten things up on the Forum and I like to think it was sort of an initiation that helped make me a part of the CI Nucleus Forum circle of friends. In the two years I have been a subscriber, I have met so many wonderful people. They all have one common goal either for themselves or a loved one—to hear with the cochlear implant. I have learned much about the cochlear implant and I hope the sharing of my experiences has been of help to others.

During the six months I was waiting to begin using both my Nucleus 22 and my Nucleus 24 Contour, I did not receive any invitations to give a presentation. Shortly after my Nucleus 22 was reactivated, I was invited to share my story with members of the Lutheran Brotherhood, Branch #8416, annual meeting. There were several in attendance who were hearing impaired or knew someone who might be helped by the cochlear implant. Also in attendance was a member of the Northeast Minneapolis Kiwanis Club. He extended an invitation to me to speak at their meeting in December.

In my haste to share my story of how my hearing was restored with the cochlear implant, I agreed without knowing how the Kiwanis Club helps serve the community. I went online and found out that their priority is helping children. I felt honored to be invited as I love children. Those who are deaf are dear to my heart. Now was a chance to tell them how they were being helped with the cochlear implant.

My presentation must have been well received as the program chairman asked if he could put my name on the Minneapolis Program Club. I gave my consent and for weeks after, the telephone did not stop ringing. I was booked right through the spring months. Myron did not take my calls. He left it up to me to make arrangements. The only time I handed the phone to him was when I was going to be given directions on how to get to the meeting place. Had I not done so, we would not have found our way.

When the hearing of my Nucleus 22 had stablized, I returned to the research laboratory to find that in the ten months I had been absent, many changes had occurred with my electrodes. During the process of finding my threshold and comfort levels, some electrodes became stagnant at the medium loud range. There were accompanying clicking and pinging sounds with some electrodes. Some had to be aborted, due to pain or dizziness, long before I reached the medium loud range. Even so, although the static remained, if I did not have the sensitivity turned up too high, it did not interfere with my Nucleus 24 Contour processor.

I loved the feeling of aliveness I now experienced. The most noticeable improvement with bilateral hearing was, of course, in noise. When my grandson, Jeffery, and I went for our walks, it didn't matter which side he was walking on. We conversed easily as car after car sped by.

I'm not sure if I could always tell the direction where sounds came from as sounds were higher pitched on my Nucleus 24 Contour side and lower on my Nucleus 22 side. If I heard a low pitched sound, such as a truck, I still tended to think it was on my right side. I do remember being able to follow the path of an airplane as it came from the east, passed overhead and then faded out as it flew west.

Do you remember when I mentioned that after receiving my Nucleus 22 I told my audiologist I could hear everything and then, later, feeling there was a puzzle piece missing? Well, I discovered I hadn't been hearing everything, after all. I found that there were even more wonderful things to hear. I was sure I had found more of the missing puzzle pieces when I began wearing both my processors. Music sounded more resonant and I was soon doing very well without the aid of my closed captioning on TV. But, of course, the voices of my grandchildren were the best sounds of all. The little ones were so much easier to understand.

One day, when Myron and I were visiting our son, Dave, and

his family in Buffalo, Minnesota, Brandon showed me some little rocks he had found.

I said, "Let's go find some more," and off we went to their backyard. They had just moved into their new home and it was not yet landscaped so there was a treasure chest of rocks of all sizes. I handed Brandon the little rocks and I threw the bigger ones out into the weeds. With each throw, he looked at me and said, "Oh, good throw, Grandma!"

To be able to hear those funny things was the most wonderful thing in the world. I was so thankful then, that instead of "sitting it out," I had chosen to dance.

When I thought back on the events of the previous year, memories of my high school days came to my mind. Back then, I did not think I had been given such a hard row to hoe. At the time, I did not consider the events of 2001 difficult, either. But now, after thinking it over, it was an arduous time. Had I not drawn on the gifts I received from my parents—patience, self-control and tolerance—I would not have persevered.

I had another positive thing going for me during this time. Thanks to my Nucleus 24 Contour, my hearing was so much better than it was when I was in high school. In just a few weeks, I would find out how much better it was.

# Update on Nucleus® Bilateral Cochlear Implants

*by Aaron Parkinson, M.A., Principal Clinical Studies Specialist, Cochlear Americas*

Since 2002, Cochlear™ Americas has been conducting clinical research in the United States on bilateral implantation in adults and children. The purpose is to evaluate the advantages of bilateral implantation compared to cochlear implantation in one ear through measures of speech perception and localization. Currently, in Cochlear's database there are approximately 200 bilatereal recipients (70 percent adults, 30 percent children) in the U.S.

Potential advantages of bilateral implantation include the ability to hear sounds on both sides of the head, the abililty to locate the source of various sounds in the environment and improved understanding in background noise.

## Adult Bilateral Case Study

When the initial studies began in 2002, all the participants were adults. The study, which is now complete, had 28 adult participants across 16 different cochlear implant centers.

Overall the study had very positive outcomes. The results from a questionnaire that all participants completed showed that the majority of the participants (24/26) preferred to use both cochlear implants together all the time and indicated that sound seems most pleasant and natural with both cochlear implant systems. The majority of participants "Agreed" or "Strongly Agreed" that the sound from the two systems "blend together" well and "Agree" or "Strongly Agreed" that they wre happy with their decision to receive bilateral cochlear implants.

Participants also showed significant improvements in speech

understanding in noise and in quiet in the bilateral condition. All participants demonstrated improved localization ability.

## Pediatric Bilateral Case Study

The pediatric bilateral case study, which began in 2003, is closed to new enrollments, however data is still being gathered. There are 28 children enrolled in the study across 10 cochlear implant centers in the U.S. Of these children, 6 are 3 to 5 years old; 11 are 5 to 8 years old and 11 are over the age of 8 years. None of the children received both implants at the same time, rather they received their second implant some time after the first, called sequential implantation.

Preliminary data shows, thus far, performance for the first implant side is superior to the second side in most if not all of the cases for speech in quiet. Over time, the second implant side acquires improved speech recognition closing the gap between the two ears. It appears as though younger kids may be adapting to the second ear more easily in line with the postlingual adult data, bilateral implantation appears to offer the potential for improved hearing in noise and localization. However, in contrast to the adults, localization in children is more difficult and takes longer to develop.

Adults and children do not have to participate in a bilateral case study in order to receive a second implant. If someone is interested in bilateral implantation, they should speak with their audiologist and/or surgeon about the possibility. As with unilateral implantation, there are no guarantees that insurance will cover a second implant.

"Faith is not about the present. It is not about things that you could capture right now with a camera.

Rather, it is about things in the future promised by God— and faith is certain of them."
—Jim Cymbala

# Part Three

## Never Give Up
### 2002-2003

N ever did I think, during my journey out of silence, that I would need to make such a difficult decision as the one I would soon face.

It was a stressful situation with much at stake. My faith sustained me—faith strong enough to make me realize there was something out there that could help me.

After much soul searching and many nights spent tossing and turning, I came to the conclusion that I had to be honest about my personal needs. I gave a lot of thought to my present situation and I knew I could not "sit it out." I had to continue dancing.

# Wings

*"Life begins each morning . . . each morning is the open door to a new world—new vistas, new aims, new tryings."*

Leigh Hodges

On January 16, 2002, I was back in the sound-treated room for my one-year speech perception testing with my Nucleus 24 Contour cochlear implant. A determination of the amount of benefit I was receiving with my bilateral implants was made at that time, also. I did not have an evaluation with my Nucleus 22. The scores from my pre-op Hearing in Noise Test (HINT) sentence scores of 41 and 26 percent were used.

The test scores using my Nucleus 24 Contour were considerably better. Without competing noise, my score was 94 percent. With noise piped in, my score dropped to 80 percent. Using both my Nucleus 22 and my Nucleus 24 Contour, my score was 96 percent without competing noise. When noise was piped in, my score dropped to 86 percent.

As you can see, the greatest improvement with my bilateral implants was in noise. General improvements were more pronounced when I was going about my normal routine and didn't think about where the speaker was situated.

When I went out to lunch with my friends, I could hear each one—not just the one who sat on my left. It was also easy to have a three-way conversation. I could have a friend on each side and hear everything that was being said. When I went to a high school basketball game, I no longer needed to avoid speaking to anyone.

I sat on a bleacher among the fans and could understand them over the din in the gym.

Our nine-year-old grandson, Jeffery, brought Myron and me to our first high school basketball game after our sons graduated. The city basketball team he played on performed at halftime. It was very noisy when we entered the gym—not at all like the silence that met me when we went to our sons' games. The pep band was playing loudly. In all the years we had attended the games, this was the first time I heard the band.

When the National Anthem was played, tears began rolling down my cheeks. Throughout the evening, the band played several songs. On the way home, Myron told me they had played them just for me. They were the same songs he had heard them play 15 years previously.

I know for a fact that listening to the band, hearing the words of the cheerleaders and the cheering of the fans was more exciting than watching the game. I couldn't concentrate on the action on the court. My eyes roamed over the gym in search of what I was hearing. I don't even remember if the Spring Lake Park Panthers won that night.

As I write my odyssey, I am convinced things do not just happen. I feel there is a plan for me and a time for everything. If Rosemary had not urged me to get on the Internet and subscribe to the Nucleus Forum, I would have missed a very special opportunity.

In late January, I received an e-mail from Cochlear Americas inviting me to apply for a position as a volunteer advocate. I wasn't at all confident that I would be selected. I knew there were others far more qualified but I completed the questionnaire and returned it. Then, I sat back and waited to find out if I had been accepted. Rosemary had also been contacted and was as anxious as I to become a volunteer. During the time spent waiting, many e-mails flew back and forth between us, asking "Have you heard anything yet?"

The long awaited e-mail arrived on February 18. The message began, "Welcome to the Nucleus Advocate Program." I had been accepted! I don't remember if Rosemary received my good news first or if I heard from her first. We were both going to be advocates.

The meeting was scheduled for April 11. I had to book my own flight which sent me into a spin. I had never flown before. Now, how was I going to get to Denver? It didn't take me long to come up with the perfect solution. Myron could fly with me. However, when I approached him with my plan, he frowned on it. Oh, well, I had plenty of time to figure something out.

I had met Julie from Wisconsin at the CIAI Convention in Minneapolis and we had been e-mailing back and forth. We had also met for lunch a couple times. I wondered if she had been invited but I hesitated to ask her for fear she had not received an invitation. Soon I found out she had been wondering if I was invited but she didn't just wonder, she acted. I received an e-mail from her telling me she was going to Denver and she asked if I was going. When I e-mailed her that I had been invited, she offered to make our travel arrangements. We would fly together on April 11.

I was very uneasy about flying but nothing was going to keep me from becoming an advocate. While I waited, I kept busy trying to keep my mind off the upcoming flight. My mornings were filled with my job at school and my afternoons were spent answering questions posted on the on-line forum and sharing my experiences with candidates.

I was invited to give a presentation at the Golden Valley Optimist Club meeting. It could not have been a more appropriate group for me to share my story. The club's motto is "Friend of

Youth." It is a service organization made up of men and women whose goal is to serve the youth in their community.

Not only was I able to tell them that I was involved with children but I told them that those who were deaf were being helped with the cochlear implant. I stressed how important it is to remain optimistic while going through the process of having the cochlear implant and the adjustment period following activation. Again, there were several in the audience who knew someone they thought could benefit from a cochlear implant.

By the time April 11 arrived, I had come to terms with myself about flying and I was ready for another adventure. The reason I would not fly was not because of the fear the plane might crash. The real fear factor had been my deafness. I lacked the confidence to try new things. Now that I could hear, I was so much more aware of my surroundings. This went a long way in giving me confidence.

My son, Scott, drove me to the airport. He gave me a confidence test immediately on arrival there. Instead of accompanying me to the ticket window, he let me go alone. He stood in the background ready to assist me if I needed help.

Since the 9/11 attack on the New York City Trade Center, the security was tighter. Everything went well until the ticket agent asked me, "Has anyone other than you touched your luggage since you arrived at the airport?"

I thought for a second. Yes, Scott had carried it in. I answered, "Yes."

The agent looked at me and was about to say something. Scott had overheard our exchange and told the agent, "No."

I received my ticket and Julie and I headed for the security check. After my encounter with the security check when Myron and I picked up my brother and sister-in-law the previous winter, I was apprehensive about going through it again. Since it was my

*Dora shared the importance of being optimistic in regaining her hearing with a cochlear implant to members of the Golden Valley (Minnesota) Optimist Club.*

Nucleus 24 Contour that had set it off, I would turn that processor off and just have my Nucleus 22 on. It worked. I breezed right through!

Julie and I found our gate. We both had a problem understanding everything through the intercom so we went to the desk and asked the agent to tell us when it was time for us to board. Then, we relaxed while we waited.

My favorite part of the flight was takeoff. It was totally awesome. I watched out the window as everything sped by. Then the plane was off the ground and soon the buildings and cars had shrunk out of sight and we were up in the clouds. I had not seen a more beautiful sight.

Descending from the clouds was also awesome. The farm fields were spread out in a patchwork quilt tapestry. Myron has a picture of an aerial view of his grandparents' farm. It is beautiful, also, but I saw this picture unfold in living color. Touchdown was exciting as we watched the wind flaps on the wings when the plane descended. Soon there was a thud and the wheels touched the ground. We had landed.

It was great to meet the staff of Cochlear Americas and fellow advocates who had come from throughout the United States. The time I spent in Denver was filled to the brim with fellowship, sightseeing and, above all, learning about the Nucleus device.

It was back to the airport on Sunday morning to catch our flight home. For some reason, I thought of the Lion, the Scarecrow and the Tin Man from the book, *The Wizard of Oz*. The Scarecrow went to Oz seeking a brain, the Tin Man searched for a heart, and the cowardly Lion wanted courage. I did have a heart and when I boarded the plane, it was filled with wonderful memories of my new friends and good times spent in beautiful Colorado. I also had a brain and that was filled with so much information about the Nucleus Cochlear implant. Like the cowardly Lion, I had wanted courage. I found it with my cochlear implants. They had given me wings.

# Blessing in Disguise

*"You have to believe the buds will grow
Believe in the grass in the days of snow.
Ah, that's the reason a bird can sing.
On the darkest day, he believes in Spring."*
                                    —Author Unknown

O n May 23, I received my Nucleus 24 Contour ESPrit 3G, a behind-the-ear processor compatible with my Nucleus 24 Contour implant. Recently, I found a notebook in which I had written the following about my activation day.

My audiologist first programmed my Nucleus 24 Contour BWP. The sound was so good that I was reluctant to give it up for my Nucleus 24 Contour ESPrit 3G but it was now or never. I thought that if I didn't like it, I could always go back to using my BWP. It took only a few minutes to place the ACE strategy at 900 Hz, one with sensitivity setting and one with volume, in the two slots and it was ready to go. After I placed the batteries in the battery compartment, I turned the program selection on sensitivity. After I turned on the processor, I was on the air.

My audiologist began speaking and I began laughing. Her voice had changed. It had become very sophisticated. I switched to the volume setting, and she was back to sounding like herself.

As I left the sound-treated room, I heard "Anesthesia stat needed on four," come over the loudspeaker. I was so surprised as that was the first time I had heard a message as clearly as that.

As I walked through the tunnel leading to the hospital, I could understand the voices of those passing by. Two gals were walking together. Then, as they parted, one said, "I'm going downstairs. You meet me there."

When I stood in the entrance of the hospital waiting for Myron to pick me up, I heard the beeps of the shuttles as they were being backed up. There is an elevator off to the side of the entrance that takes visitors down to the level leading to the parking ramp. The bell had always sounded so harsh. Today it was so much mellower.

I had written down volume control and disposable batteries as the features I liked the best. I still like the convenience of using disposable batteries but now I prefer the sensitivity setting over volume, perhaps it is because I had used it on my Nucleus 22 for so long. I soon added other features to the list.

We purchased a telecoil adaptable telephone for our den. It was great not to have to ask the caller to hold while I plugged the adapter into my processor. I only had to switch on the telecoil as I walked to the den. Then, I picked up the receiver and said, "Hello." Voices came through loud and clear.

After a few days, Myron dismantled the Nucleus 24 Contour telephone adapter from our kitchen phone and reconnected the Nucleus 22 adapter. I still could not hear on the telephone with my Nucleus 22 but I wanted it there should my hearing improve.

The colored battery covers were another feature I liked about the Nucleus 24 Contour ESPrit 3G. When I first saw the 12 different colors, I thought I would give them away to someone younger. One day, I matched the yellow cover with a yellow T-shirt I was wearing and thought it looked very stylish. That was the beginning of

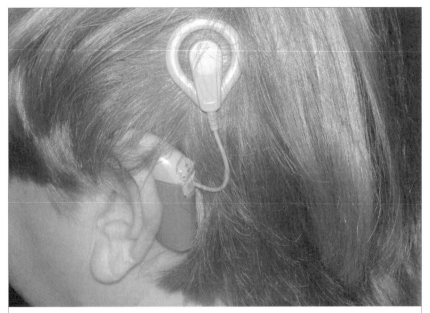

*Dora's Nucleus 24 Contour ESPrit 3G*

Grandma's fun. The colors poking out from under my hair looked pretty cool. The children at Olive Tree thought so, too.

I noticed a big improvement in the sound at Olive Tree the first day I wore my Nucleus 24 Contour ESPrit 3G. The children were much quieter. I was able to understand a student's request so much easier. In fact, for the first time all year, I was able to understand requests without having to ask the child to step out into the quiet hall. I had not intended to return the following fall but now that I was hearing so much better, I reconsidered. I signed my contract for the school year beginning August 25, 2002.

Much of my summer was spent outside just listening to the sounds of nature and the neighborhood. I was continually experimenting while out on my walks or just relaxing on my deck. I had fun playing hide and seek with the birds. When I heard a bird sing, I would try to find it. If I took either processor off, it was on the side of the processor that I had left on. With both processors on, I could usually pinpoint the tree the bird was sitting in. Then, I would watch and soon the bird would fly out of the tree.

I also learned to tell which neighbor was mowing his lawn. I already knew where the train track was located so I just used the whistle to test the loudness of my processors. It was louder and clearer with my Nucleus 24 ESPrit 3G. With my Nucleus 22, it was not as loud and there was a gravelly sound to it. With both processors, the sound was very full and natural sounding.

Throughout the summer, I returned to have my Nucleus 22 reprogrammed several times. For a time after the programming, the sound seemed to have improved. Now I wonder if it really was better or if it was because I wanted it to so much that I imagined it to be better. After a few days, the sound was not good again. It was in the fall when I returned to Olive Tree that I realized just how much the sound had changed.

Olive Tree was going to be in a different room that year. It was smaller but more compact with built-in cupboards along the back of the room and with shelves to hold the many books that had accumulated over the years. The week before school was to resume, I went there to get everything organized.

There were boxes of toys, books and games scattered throughout the room. It was nice to have a place to put everything and I was going to see that the room stayed neat. Now that I had a year's experience, I felt more confident. I was going to instill in the children the saying, "A place for everything and everything in its place." It took only one day to dash my confidence.

As it had been at the beginning of the previous school year, it was impossible to understand the children. I could not discern a simple request to get a drink of water without asking them to step out in the hallway where it was quiet. I tried hard the first week but no matter how much adjusting I did with my processors, it didn't help. I was back to spending most of the time standing out in the hall, looking in on the children.

I knew I could not continue like this. The children needed someone who could understand them. I realized I could not handle the job and gave my notice on Friday, agreeing to stay until September 15.

I spent the following two weeks explaining to the children and the teachers that the reason for my leaving was not because the children were naughty or unusually noisy. It was because it was difficult for me to hear in any noise. A replacement was found and she visited with us the last Thursday and Friday I was there. I was confident the children were in good hands.

I did miss "my kids." I walked to the school several times that fall to attend Wednesday morning Chapel and I often stayed to have lunch with them. When they saw me come walking down the hall, many of the little ones would shout, "Dora!" and come running to give me a big hug. Tears still come to my eyes when I remember one little girl who told me, "I will tell the kids to be quiet if you will come back."

In the year I spent with them, I had grown to love them. I had not thought they would return that love. They were often in my thoughts and I frequently dreamed I was back with them. For one short moment, while I was on vacation, I thought they were with me.

Ever since I had taken my first flight to Denver, I had been waiting for the time when I could fly again. This time, I wanted Myron to accompany me. When our son, Scott, suggested that the three of us fly to Seattle and take the ferry to Victoria, British Columbia, I said, "Let's go!" Scott made the reservations.

On arriving in Seattle, we spent the night at the elegant, restored turn-of-the-century Pioneer Square Hotel. It was only a short distance from the Washington State Ferry Terminal where the ferry which was to take us to Victoria was docked .

After going through customs, we boarded the ferry and waited for it to depart. As usual, I was thinking about Olive Tree. When I heard voices of children, I thought I was imagining them. When they grew louder, I turned around and saw boys and girls, all neatly dressed in uniforms, walking down the aisle. They took seats right across from us.

A chaperone sat across the aisle from me and I couldn't resist asking about the children. They were from a parochial school in Seattle and were on a field trip to Victoria. For a time, I wondered if their chatter would bother me but I soon found out that I did not need to worry. They took out their notebooks and pencils and were engrossed in writing during the entire trip.

We had a wonderful time in Victoria. We spent most of our visit in Old Town Victoria, a quaint little town which has many heritage buildings from the turn of the century. We spent much time in the shops and strolling along the streets.

I heard the birds singing there, too. There were trees planted at each crossing. Just as we were about to step off the curb, I heard a bird singing merrily. I glanced over my shoulder to see if I could see it. Just like the birds back home, they hid from me. The same thing happened at the next corner. I wanted to linger but Myron and Scott hurried me on. At the next corner, it happened again.

This time, Scott said, "The birds are on the signal light."

I looked but couldn't see them. Then he started to laugh and asked me, "When do you hear them?"

I said, "When we start to cross the street."

Then I caught on. Whenever the light turned green, the bird sang. I thought that made for a cheery little greeting. I felt pretty humble when Scott explained it was to help the blind cross the street. Had I not been able to hear with my cochlear implant, I could still safely cross but if I had been blind, I would not have

*Dora and Myron by the Victoria, British Columbia wharf*

seen the light when it changed to green. The birds singing tell the blind when it is safe to cross.

We spent one morning at the beautiful Butchart Gardens where we saw the Sunken Garden, the Japanese and Italian Gardens and acres of every flower imaginable. We spent the evenings and the morning before our departure walking on Wharf Street where the beautiful heritage homes are now shops and restaurants.

On the morning before our return to Seattle, Myron and I were tired so we wanted to relax down by the wharf. Scott went off exploring by himself. He had not been gone long when we saw him come running and motioning for us to follow him.

We just made it to Wharf Street in time to see a Canadian military group, in traditional uniforms of kilts, come marching down the street.

I don't know if they were playing any other instruments because all I heard were the bagpipes. I have never heard so many bagpipes played at one time nor seen such precision marching.

We had been given so many surprises while we were there and we weren't to leave before we had one more. As we were waiting to board the ferry for our trip back to Seattle, I noticed a group of girls waiting to board. I was surprised when I saw "Australia" embroidered on the back of their jackets. They sat right in front of us.

Of course, my curiosity got the best of me. I leaned over and asked the girl who was sitting in front of me where they were headed. In heavily accented English, she told me the group was a soccer team from Sydney and were going to the States to compete in a tournament.

Oh, how I loved the sound of her voice. I could have talked longer but she was tired. I did tell her about my cochlear implant and asked her if she was familiar with it or with Professor Graeme Clark and the development of the Australian multiple-electrode cochlear implant (bionic ear). Unfortunately, she wasn't but she said she would remember to investigate it when she returned home.

When we returned home, I had more surprises and both proved that my resigning from Olive Tree was a blessing. While we were gone, the Day Care provider for our grandsons, Jeffery and Justin, had given her notice. The boys needed someone to care for them before and after school. I stepped in. I didn't have the problems understanding them that I had with the children in Olive Tree and all went well.

Most mornings we spent sitting in the rocker just talking. I told them stories of when I was a little girl and sometimes we were just silly. Justin still liked to laugh and he did his utmost to make me laugh, too. The hour after school was spent playing outdoors. I taught them how to play Captain, May I?, Blind Man's Bluff, and tree tag. Jeffery had grown into a very competitive, athletic fourth grader. His favorite "game" was participating in the Olympics. Jeffery and Justin ran and jumped while I recorded their statistics.

Later that fall, I began to once again experience fullness around the site of my Nucleus 22 implanted receiver and in my ear canal. It was more pronounced than it had been previously. I also began to experience pain in my eyetooth on the side of my implanted Nucleus 22.

Another visit was made to the clinic where I was reprogrammed. Two electrodes were found to be causing the pain and were deactivated. I was then down to eight active electrodes. The sounds became more distorted but I continued to wear my processor. If I had the sensitivity set on Number One, it did not interfere with the hearing I received with my Nucleus 24 Contour ESPrit 3G.

One morning, a couple of weeks later, when I put my Nucleus 22 processor on, there was pain in all my teeth, upper and lower, that were on the side of my Nucleus 22. There was also pain radiating up that side of my face. My right arm was also affected. My audiologist was on vacation so while I waited for her return, I wore my Nucleus 22 sparingly.

I was back to the clinic the day she returned. Again, I was reprogrammed. No more electrodes were deactivated but my comfort level was turned down until I could no longer feel the pain in my teeth. I had to have my sensitivity turned up to Number Five but, even then, sound was very distorted. I was to return for speech testing to assess the amount of benefit I was receiving from my Nucleus 22. Unless things changed drastically, I knew I would not do well. I left the clinic with tears running down my cheeks; I was devastated. I did not want to lose my Nucleus 22.

# The Right Decision

I spent the next few weeks doing much soul searching. When I was a little girl, I had a friend named Karen. Whenever she heard me say that I loved an object, she would admonish me. It did not matter if it was a favorite candy bar, a book, or even my favorite song, "You Are My Sunshine." She would tell me I couldn't love something that didn't have a heart to love me back.

Well, heart or no heart, I had fallen in love with my Nucleus 22 cochlear implant. The VIP (Very Important Processor) sticker that had been placed on the Dry Aid Pack, prior to my Nucleus 24 Contour implant surgery, was still there. Every night, before going to bed, when I placed my processor in the bag, I was reminded of the years of happiness it had brought to me. I could not give it up without trying one more time.

I did not want to leave my present clinic where everyone and everything was familiar to me. But I could not ignore my feelings for my Nucleus 22. It was very valuable to me and I could not give it up until the last shred of sound was gone. The memories of the good hearing I had once received with it and the "surround sound" hearing experience at the activation of my Nucleus 24 Contour remained with me.

Those memories inspired me to ask Pastor Strawn for guidance. He was not about to tell me what to do. I would have to find out on my own. He did tell me I should not dwell on the "whys" of the past and I should not look into the future. I should concentrate on the "now"; if I let God lead me, everything would work out.

I returned for several more chats and with each one, it became clearer that this was a part of God's plan for me. If I was to regain the hearing with my Nucleus 22, I would have to take the stumbling block placed in my path and turn it into one more stepping stone. I would have to keep trying so I decided to seek another opinion elsewhere.

At the CIAI Convention in Minneapolis in July of 2001, I visited with Dr. Jon Shallop, a cochlear implant audiologist at the Mayo Clinic in Rochester, Minnesota. In the few minutes we had chatted, I discovered he had a keen interest in research of the cochlear implant.

The memory of that visit, along with the 1985 revisal stapedectomy I had undergone at the Mayo Clinic, helped me decide to return there. I would be on familiar territory and I knew that was where I was meant to go. I contacted the clinic and an appointment was scheduled for January 31, only three weeks away.

Never did I think, while talking with Dr. Shallop at the convention, that I would someday be in his office, talking with him across his desk. We spent some time getting acquainted and I answered his questions about my Nucleus 22.

Then, it was time to get to work. He said he would begin by giving me an integrity test (see page 205). I had seen posts regarding this test on the Nucleus Forum and often wondered if the test would benefit me. Now, here I was, looking at the machine and about to be hooked up to it.

Dr. Shallop explained what it does but the technical terms flew right over my head. I became quite apprehensive, my mind racing ahead to what the results would show. Would he be able to help me? I knew I would be disappointed if there was nothing more that could be done. However, I also knew I would have the satisfaction of knowing I had tried.

First, Dr. Shallop hooked me up to the integrity machine by putting small disk electrodes in place. They resembled those used when I had electrocardiograms before both of my implant surgeries. Only this time, instead of placing them on my chest and back, they were positioned in various places on my head. He explained that these would measure the signals of each electrode. The patterns of the graphs, which resembled those during an electrocardiogram, would reveal any problems I was having with my electrodes.

My Nucleus 24 Contour was chosen to be tested first. Many times, when being programmed, I had listened to the "beep, beep, beep" of my electrodes as they were brought up to my comfort level. I had never seen them on the computer although often I wondered what that looked like.

Now, I was seeing, first hand, just how they acted. The best way I can describe them is that they danced across the screen in perfect symmetry. The only electrodes that caused facial stimulation were Numbers 14, 15, 16 and 17, the same ones that had been deactivated during my initial stimulation.

The rest of my electrodes were well proportioned and well balanced. There was no interruption in the intermittence of the electrodes and all tests were within normal limits. The results were very different with the electrodes of my Nucleus 22.

We were not far into the testing of my Nucleus 22 when the twitching and dizziness began. Although there was no facial stimulation when the first four electrodes were tested, the next 14 electrodes caused much dizziness and twitching. I thought I would fall off my chair and my face felt like it was being twisted out of shape.

I did not spend much time looking at the screen but when I did, it looked as though my electrodes were sizzling. There was no stimulation with the last four electrodes. When Dr. Shallop said we were finished and began to remove the electrodes from my head, I felt relieved. As he removed them, he made two comments.

He looked at me and said, "You have otosclerosis, Dora."

Dr. Shallop also said it was unfortunate that the Nucleus 24 Contour was not available when I was implanted with my Nucleus 22 and explained what he meant.

The same electrodes, Numbers 14, 15, 16, and 17, that caused problems with my Nucleus 24 Contour, had caused the same problems with my Nucleus 22. He said that, quite likely, this is where my cochleas are the most porous. It is here where my cochleas are closest to my facial nerve. The electrical current escapes at this point, hits my facial nerve and causes twitching or dizziness. If I had been implanted with another Nucleus 22 in my left ear, Dr. Shallop explained, perhaps I would have had the same experience with facial stimulation as I was having with my right implant.

The Nucleus 24 Contour implant is a self-curling electrode array that places each stimulating electrode close to the inner wall of the cochlea where the nerve cells are located. This also places the electrodes as far away from the facial nerve as possible. Thus, only four electrodes caused facial stimulation and had to be deactivated.

The more he explained, the more I felt that the Nucleus 22 problems were insurmountable and that he could not help me. I began to prepare myself to hear the bad news. Yes, I had come with hope that I would find a solution to my problems and it made me sad to think that the hope was dashed. Yet, I did not feel that my clinic visit was a waste of my time. I found out what I wanted to know—what was happening with my electrodes.

I thought my visit was about to come to an end and my mind began to wander. I began to reconcile myself to being without my Nucleus 22. As I began to gather up my belongings in preparation for leaving, I heard Dr. Shallop say he was going to MAP me. That caught my attention and I sat up straight. He moved his chair over to his computer and turned it on. My entire body broke out in goosebumps. There was still hope for my Nucleus 22.

# Impossible Dream

When Dr. Shallop began to explain how he was going to attempt to get more electrodes activated on my Nucleus 22 implant, I found it very difficult to concentrate on what he was saying. All I could think about was that there was still hope for my Nucleus 22. It was going to be given another chance. About all I remember him saying was that he was going to get the electrical current to flow away from the point in my cochlea where I was experiencing facial stimulation. After reading a copy of the clinical document, explaining the program in more detail, it became clearer to me.

By using variable mode programming, Dr. Shallop was able to get the electrical current flowing away from the middle turn of my cochlea where I was getting facial stimulation and dizziness. Before he began, he deactivated electrodes Number 12, 13, 14 and 15, the electrodes that caused the most facial stimulation. By using variations of modes, he proceeded to program the remaining top electrodes, Number 16 to 21, which are the high pitched electrodes. I was able to take them up to a usable comfort level without experiencing any facial stimulation or dizziness. My electrodes rang clear and true.

Dr. Shallop then proceeded, in the same way, with electrode Number 11. He shifted the current of electrodes Number 10 through Number 2 so it would flow toward electrode Number 1. Once again, I successfully brought the electrodes up to a usable comfort level without experiencing facial stimulation or dizziness. My "bullfrog" and the banging and clanging I had been experiencing recently had disappeared. When the programming was finished, I had 16 active electrodes, twice the number I had when I entered his office.

Now that Dr. Shallop had the electrodes programmed, it was time to balance the loudness. The same procedure I was familiar with was used. First, I listened to three electrodes, then six, etc. When all the electrodes seemed to be of the same loudness, he told me he would do the "sweep" of all 16 electrodes. All the while Dr. Shallop was programming my Nucleus 22, he sat bent over his computer, in deep concentration. Then, he pushed his chair back, folded his hands in his lap and waited for me to respond.

I smile as I think about what I heard. It was like someone running their fingers down a piano keyboard, one key at a time. All the electrodes were in tune. It sounded so nice that I asked to hear them over and over, first frontwards and then backwards. When I had heard them enough, my processor was unplugged from the computer and a battery was placed in the battery compartment. Before turning on the switch, Dr. Shallop cautioned me the sound would not be like I had once heard it because of variable mode programming.

I was more optimistic. Since the electrodes were pitched so perfectly, I expected the sound to be like it had been prior to having my Nucleus 24 Contour implanted.

When Dr. Shallop turned on the processor and began to speak, I was surprised. I could understand him but his voice was very squeaky. Myron spoke and his voice was not the familiar sounding voice. His, too, was squeaky. Dr. Shallop told me the sound would improve with time and said I should put on my Nucleus 24 Contour ESPrit 3G. I did and the sounds of my two processors blended beautifully. I did not notice the squeakiness of my Nucleus 22. I was told to return in one month for more mapping.

I don't think I had been as happy when either my Nucleus 22 or my Nucleus 24 Contour was activated than I was when I left Dr. Shallop's office that day. I had come so close to losing my Nucleus 22 that it had become extra joyful. It was like starting over with another implant. I kept a journal for the first month after my Nucleus 22 was reprogrammed and I want to share some entries with you.

*My Journal*

**Saturday, February 1**—The sounds with my Nucleus 22 are very squeaky and squished. Myron and I went to the mall to walk this morning. The sounds in the mall were annoying and I planned to avoid talking to anyone. When I met a friend, I couldn't shun her so I stopped to talk with her. I had a little problem understanding her because sounds with my Nucleus 22 were still squeaky and squished. I was able to understand when she told me there was a problem with the space shuttle Columbia. When we returned home, I turned TV on and heard the sad news. The Columbia had disintegrated 15 minutes before the scheduled landing at the Kennedy Space Center in Florida. Later in the day, I heard President Bush say, in a televised address, "The Columbia is lost. There are no survivors."

**Sunday, February 2**—Myron and I went to our grandson Jacob's first communion. I wore both my Nucleus 22 and my Nucleus 24 Contour ESPrit 3G. The organ music was very nice. There was also a bell choir and ringing bells sounded so pretty. I think it was the first time I had heard a bell choir live. Halfway through the song, the battery of my Nucleus 22 went dead. Much of the good sound was taken away.

I had left my extra batteries in the car so I had to rely on hearing the sermon with my Nucleus 24 Contour ESPrit 3G. I heard the pastor quite well. Then, my Nucleus 24 Contour ESPrit 3G shut off. I didn't have batteries along for that processor, either, but I turned it off for a few minutes and then switched it back on. Sound returned.

I changed the battery of my Nucleus 22 in the car on the way to our son's house but I had forgotten to bring batteries along for my Nucleus 24 Contour ESPrit 3G. I was worried that the batteries would go dead before the day was over but they lasted until we were about ready to leave for home. Sounds with my Nucleus 22 were not good so I was happy when we reached home and I could put fresh batteries in my Nucleus 24 Contour ESPrit 3G.

**Monday, February 3**—I put my Nucleus 24 Contour ESPrit 3G on first this morning. Later, while listening to my CDs on the stereo, I put my Nucleus 22 on. The music definitely sounded better while wearing both processors.

**Tuesday, February 4**—Today is Myron's and my 42nd wedding anniversary.

I started the day wearing both processors. I heard the ticking of the clock in our kitchen for the first time. The water running from the faucet is not so squeaky and neither is the sound when I clear my throat. When I take my Nucleus 22 processor off, all the sound is on my left side. When I take my Nucleus 24 Contour ESPrit 3G off, the sound is on my right side. When I have both processors on, the sound is at the center of my head.

**Tuesday, February 18**—A Christmas gift, the first year after I received my Nucleus 22 implant, was a bird clock from Myron. A different bird sings each hour on the hour. This morning I was sitting in the kitchen when the kingfisher belted out his song at 9:00 a.m. I had time to listen with each processor separately. The song sounded much the same with each one. I watched a memorial to the shuttle Columbia later in the day. The battery of my Nucleus 22 went dead and my hearing went down. I hurried to put in a fresh battery. I was able to understand the speeches and songs quite well without the use of closed captioning.

**Wednesday, February 19**—I am down in the basement computer room. I hear so many more knocking and squeaking sounds I have not heard before. It is kind of scary. I really had a scare this morning. All of a sudden, I heard a loud rumble. Thinking that the furnace was about to blow up, I jumped up from my chair and hurried up the steps and went outdoors. When nothing happened, I gingerly made my way back down to the basement and peeked into the laundry room. Our washing machine was half way across the room. I had put an extra heavy load of clothes in to wash. The clothes became unbalanced and the machine had danced across the floor.

**Thursday, February 20**—Myron and I had dinner at Ruby Tuesdays. We had been there several times after I began having problems with my Nucleus 22. I had heard the music then but it had not sounded pleasant. This evening I heard it like music should be heard. I didn't have any problems placing my order and Myron and I were able to converse easily over the background sounds of people talking and dishes clattering.

**Saturday, February 21**—I spent three hours in the school gym watching basketball games. I didn't have any problems visiting with friends.

**Sunday, February 22**—Myron and I sat in the back of the church where the organ pipes are located. Just like the first Sunday after my Nucleus 22 was activated, the organ was very loud. I turned the sensitivity down on both processors but it was still too loud. My Nucleus 24 Contour kept going off. Finally, I just left it off and listened with my Nucleus 22. The sound was not nearly as good and I had to turn the sensitivity up to Number Five.

I switched my Nucleus 24 Contour ESPrit 3G back on after the service was over and I decided to stay for Bible Study. The lesson was interesting but something else was, also. When Pastor Strawn leads the study, he does not stay in one spot. He moves around the room. My "ears" followed him wherever he went and I was able to understand him well. I am so thankful to have my Nucleus 22 back and to, once again, be experiencing surround sound.

# Squeaky Hollow

*"God sometimes makes mountains one
pebble at a time."*
                                        —Author Unknown

The next week, while I was waiting to return to the clinic for an assessment and further programming, I spent a lot of time testing the sounds with only my Nucleus 22. Just as Dr. Shallop predicted, my understanding of speech had become easier but everything still sounded squeaky. A hollowness had set in, also. I began to call the MAP I had received, "Squeaky Hollow." I was hopeful that when I returned to the clinic at the end of the week, something could be done to get rid of the squeaks and the hollow sound.

When I returned to the clinic on Friday and told Dr. Shallop about "Squeaky Hollow," he thought that was a descriptive way of explaining how my MAP sounded. He set to work trying to get rid of the squeaks and hollowness. Instead of going through the process of finding the threshold and comfort levels of each electrode, he reviewed the program I had received on January 31 and decided to make a few changes. On my previous MAP, he had double mapped two of my channels. He changed this so all my electrodes were independent and now each electrode was being stimulated one after another. When this was done, Dr. Shallop did some "tweaking" with my program.

As he worked, he had me listen to two different sounds. When I heard each one, I was to describe it. This was very difficult for me to do as I had never been asked to do so before. I pretty much stuck with "squeaky" and "hollow." I used Myron's voice as a tester.

His voice never reached the level of what it had once been with my Nucleus 22. We just stopped when I thought it sounded the best. He did get rid of the hollow sound but the squeakiness remained.

I had not been thinking about having word and sentence tests that day so I was taken by surprise when Dr. Shallop said he would like to do some testing. This had always been a part of the cochlear implant process I did not look forward to. I always made appointments to have yearly evaluations. By the time the day of my appointment arrived, I was very nervous, so being caught off guard as I was this time was very beneficial. I did not have time to think about it. We went right to the sound treated room and went to work.

The scores of the word tests were 20 percent with my Nucleus 22, 44 percent with my Nucleus 24 Contour ESPrit 3G. Using both my Nucleus 22 and my Nucleus 24 Contour ESPrit 3G, my score was 58 percent. My sentence scores were 42 percent with my Nucleus 22; 84 percent with my Nucleus 24 Contour ESPrit 3G and 95 percent with both processors together.

My test scores clearly showed I did better in the binaural condition. Even though the scores with my Nucleus 24 Contour ESPrit 3G were higher than those with my Nucleus 22, I was very happy with the scores I received with my Nucleus 22. One month before, I was not getting any usable hearing with my Nucleus 22. Now, I was understanding close to half of what I heard. I was not experiencing any facial stimulation or dizziness and the feeling of fullness around the site of the receiver was less severe. In just one month, there had been a great improvement. I was confident that my hearing would continue to get better over time.

My hearing did improve but the squeakiness persisted. I did not like it. I began to notice it even when I was wearing both processors. It became so obsessive that it was on my mind most of the time. One day, I was putting on my coat, getting ready to go for my morning walk and as I zipped up the zipper, I got all excited. I actually talked to myself.

I said, "Hey, the zipper sounds exactly like the squeaks I have been hearing!"

I couldn't wait to tell Dr. Shallop when I returned to the clinic for another assessment in March. He had heard sound described in many ways but this was the first time a recipient had described it to him as sounding like a zipper.

He did some more tweaking and soon the zipper sound disappeared. Another evaluation was done. My word comprehension score had risen to 28 percent and the score I received listening to sentences had risen to 47 percent. Best of all, when I left the clinic, the sound was pretty much on a par to what it was like prior to having my Nucleus 24 Contour implanted.

That spring went by fast. We were kept busy with our grandkids' school and sports activities. Jeffery, Jacob, Justin and Chelsea were all playing soccer. Jeffery was again in the Math Bowl and he went on to the District Spelling Bee. I was able to hear the words the students were to spell but I could not always hear the students as they spelled them although I was able to hear and understand Jeffery well. I applauded when he spelled the word correctly and anguished as he struggled to spell those words unfamiliar to him. He did not win a ribbon but he did a great job. Grandpa and I were proud of him.

May was a very busy month. When I heard there were plans to start a Cochlear Implant Club at the Mayo Cochlear Implant Facility, I offered to help. A spring group educational meeting was being planned for May. I had met Bev, the chairman, at a gathering of the CIAI Minnesota group. She and I began working together.

Invitations to all patients and other interested groups were sent out. There was a very good turnout. The meeting was an all-day affair. Representatives from all three cochlear implant companies gave presentations. A social hour was held over lunch. It was a success. We received many requests for another get-together the following spring. It was a great opportunity for me to become acquainted with new cochlear implant recipients.

We also attended our granddaughter Chelsea's dance recital in May. The dancing and costumes were so beautiful and the recital had all the earmarks of professionalism. Chelsea looked so grownup with her hair piled up on top of her head. It was cute to see her dancing with her partner, a young man.

Most of the music was loud rock but when the little tots came out on the floor, my heart melted. It took me awhile before I understood the song they were dancing to. When I did and could actually understand the words, tears came to my eyes. It was the song, "Do-Re-Mi," from the musical *The Sound of Music* by Richard Rodgers and Oscar Hammerstein II.

Way back in 1965, when I was wearing hearing aids, I went to the movie with a group of neighbor gals. Then, I could not understand all the lyrics. The only lines I was able to understand were, "Do, a deer, a female deer" and "Mi, the name I call myself."

Now I heard everything so clearly. I heard that "Re" is not a drop of falling sun. It is a drop of golden sun and that "So" is a needle pulling thread and "Ti" is a drink with jam and bread.

At the end of May, our grandson, Brandon, graduated from pre-kindergarten. The pre-school, Noah's Ark, that he and his sister, Ashley, attend is a fantastic school. The children attend two years and at the end of the second year, there is a graduation ceremony. First, there is a musical program presented by both three- and four-year-olds. It was so nice to be able to hear the words and not just watch as the little ones did the hand motions.

Just before the end of the program, the graduates left the

room. When they returned, they were all decked out in graduation gowns and caps. Oh, how proud they looked! They stood at attention as they waited for their name to be called. When they heard their name, they walked up to their teacher and she presented them with a diploma. I was pretty happy when I was able to hear his teacher call "Brandon Weber" so clearly.

In July, I returned to the clinic for another assessment. The scores of my word test remained at 28 percent but my sentence score had risen three percent. It was now at 51 percent. Localization testing was also done. Three bursts of white noise were presented from either the right, left or both speakers simultaneously. Using my Nucleus 22 alone, I heard the sound on my right side regardless of which speaker the sound came from. I did the same with my Nucleus 24 Contour ESPrit 3G. With both implants on, I scored 100 percent when the noise came from the left speaker. I scored 90 percent when it came from the right speaker and 70 percent when the noise was at the center speaker. The results showed I have an advantage of using both implants for sound localization.

I did not keep a journal during this time but from time to time, I jotted down thoughts as they came to my mind. The following is what I wrote sometime during the summer:

Music is enjoyable once again and I can hear and understand much of what is said on TV without the use of closed captioning. I do believe I have found the missing puzzle piece that I went searching for in the fall of 2001. I feel now that, should something go wrong with my Nucleus 24 Contour, I could function with my Nucleus 22.

I often wonder what is down the road for me. I have long given up trying to get the Nucleus 22 ESPrit BTE but when the Nucleus ESPrit 3G becomes available, I will try to get that. Or will there come a time when my Nucleus 22 can no longer help me? Will I want to be reimplanted with another Nucleus 24 Contour or possibly a more advanced implant?

The answer is an astounding, "Yes!" Now that I have experienced surround sound to its fullest, I will do everything I can to keep it. I am now hearing like God intended for me to hear—with both ears. I am so happy I chose to dance that first dance and the second. I will continue to dance as many dances as it takes to keep the wonderful sounds that surround me.

When I wrote those words, I did not think that very soon I would come very close to losing my Nucleus 22. Once again, I would have to choose between sitting it out or dancing one more time.

# Rough and Rumbly

*"Courage doesn't always roar. Sometimes courage is the quiet voice at the end of the day saying, "I will try again tomorrow."*
—Author Unknown

It wasn't long after my Squeaky Hollow had been solved that I was confronted with other irritating sounds issuing out of my Nucleus 22. It wasn't gradual this time as it had been when my hearing began to go down with my Nucleus 22. This time, the change happened almost instantly. One day I was enjoying wonderful hearing. The next, the sounds had turned very rough and rumbly. During this time I experienced a very strange happening. I don't know if there is a connection to that and how the sounds changed or not.

One afternoon, while I was in the living room listening to my CDs, I fell asleep. Suddenly, I woke up. A loud, high pitched squealing sound was coming from somewhere. Thinking that an alarm had gone off in the house, I jumped up! I was about to go looking for the source when the sound changed into a loud clacking and banging.

Then, I thought it must be coming from one of my processors. I held the magnet of my Nucleus 22 away from my head and I did not hear it with my Nucleus 24 Contour ESPrit 3G. Then, I knew it was my Nucleus 22 processor making the terrible racket. I was about to turn the processor off when the sound began to fade away. It started up again but, this time, it was not as loud nor did it last as long. It was after this experience that I noticed there was a rough and rumbly sound to what I heard with my Nucleus 22.

At first, when I began to experience the accompanying sounds, I thought I was hearing something new in the environment. My hearing had been steadily improving since I was reprogrammed with variable mode mapping. I thought it was possible that my brain had not figured out yet what it was I was hearing. After a week or so of hearing these sounds constantly, I became frustrated. On top of this, my microphone had become very uncomfortable to wear. My receiver seemed to have dropped and perhaps worked its way out to the surface of my skin.

One morning, when I was out for my walk, my frustration increased. Not only was my microphone causing discomfort but the sounds of the passing traffic were very irritating. The birds, that had been singing so beautifully all summer, now screeched. My teeth began to hurt again. I took the microphone earpiece off my ear and let it dangle on my neck.

I have been asked why I didn't just turn my processor off. I don't have an answer for that—maybe I wanted to relieve the discomfort I was feeling. I do know that had I turned it off, I would not have noticed that the harsh, rumbling sounds disappeared, the traffic sounds became normal and the birds again sang. My teeth no longer hurt and the discomfort I had been feeling behind my ear was also relieved.

I hurried home; I wanted to do some experimenting. First, I wanted to make sure my cables were okay. I changed both the short, transmitting cable that runs from the microphone to the transmitting coil and the long headset cable that connects the speech processor to the microphone. The sound did not improve so I put the original cables back on.

After putting a CD in my boombox, I sat down to listen to the music. With the microphone earpiece in place behind my ear, music was just noise and it caused a stinging sensation in my teeth. It wasn't the same sensation I felt prior to being mapped with variable mode. It was much like I remember the feeling I had in school when a student ran a piece of chalk down the chalkboard. My teeth stung. When I took the receiver away from my ear, I heard the sound of music and could understand the lyrics easily. My teeth did not hurt.

Then, I thought I would find out if there was an improvement using my lapel microphone so I connected it to my processor. The accompanying roughness and rumble disappeared.

I was not getting a full spectrum of sounds at home so I thought I would take my experimenting to the mall. On the drive over, I kept switching my microphone. First, I would listen with it behind my ear and then hold it away from my ear.

The stretch of Highway 694 that we take to the mall has to be one of the noisiest roads in Minnesota. That morning, with my earpiece in place, it was even noisier. It sounded like we were

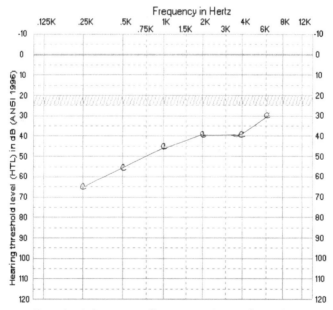

*Dora's right ear audiogram prior to her 2003*
*repositioning surgery of her Nucleus 22 implant*

speeding down an old gravel, country road. When I held the microphone away from my ear, the sounds were back to the normal, loud sounds of traffic that they had always been.

My day at the mall was very interesting. When I had the microphone in place, the sounds were so loud, I could only have the sensitivity up to Number One Half. I was surrounded by white noise and it hurt my teeth. When I held the microphone away from my ear, the sounds turned into individual sounds. I heard children laughing and crying, shoppers chatting, escalators rumbling and telephones ringing. The carts people were pushing howled when my microphone was in place but when I held it away from my ear, I heard the familiar clickety-clack of the wheels.

I had lunch at Arby's Restaurant. Again, I was surrounded by white noise when the microphone was in place. When the microphone was away from my ear, the noise changed to individual sounds. I heard the cashiers clearly, the beeping of the french fry machine, people talking and the ring of the bell as patrons rang it to show their satisfaction with the service as they left the restaurant.

After lunch, I sat on a bench near the entry to the mall. When the microphone was in place, the doors screeched when shoppers arrived and departed. Again, my teeth hurt. When I held the microphone away from my head, the screeching changed to the familiar squeaks.

I thought that was enough experimenting. I was convinced something strange was happening. It was time to contact Dr. Shallop. Appointments were scheduled with him and with Dr. Colin Driscoll, a cochlear implant surgeon at the Mayo facility.

First, Dr. Shallop did another integrity test. The results were much the same as they had been in January. Then, he got out a long cable, disconnected my microphone ear piece and connected my lapel microphone to my processor. There were inches and inches of long cables to get tangled up in and it was not as easy to find a hiding place in which to store it. That was a small price to pay as the rough and rumbly sounds disappeared.

I was off to see Dr. Driscoll. There had been changes in the otolaryngology waiting room since I had been a patient in 1985. Yet, it was like coming home after having been away for a long time. Just as it had been back then, there were many patients waiting to see their doctors. That was a sign that I would again be in good hands.

The long walk down the hallway to the examining room was familiar. Myron said the room hadn't changed but I did not remember what it had been like in 1985. There had been one big change. It was not Dr. McDonald who walked into the examining room. It was Dr. Driscoll.

After examining the site of my receiver, Dr. Driscoll sat down with Myron and me and explained his findings. He confirmed my suspicions. My receiver stimulator had migrated and was pushing on my pinna. This was the cause of the heavy feeling and the feeling of fullness in my ear canal. The rough and rumbly sounds were the results of intermittent difficulty.

I was given three options to remedy the problem:

1. I could leave the receiver as it was. When I mentioned to Dr. Driscoll that I thought the receiver had migrated as far as it could, he cautioned me, saying it could migrate farther. In addition, he told me there was a danger the receiver could, at some time, push its way through the skin.

2. I could have my Nucleus 22 removed and have a Nucleus 24 Contour reimplanted in the same ear. During our discussion of this option, he advised me that because of the calcification in my cochlea which was caused by otosclerosis, he could not guarantee he would get full insertion of my electrode.

3. I could have repositioning surgery. Dr. Driscoll would attempt to move my receiver to a different location. Once again, he cautioned me. Any bone growth where the electrode array was inserted could prevent him from successfully repositioning my receiver. The slightest movement of the wire, at the entrance of my cochlea, could shift the position of the electrodes inside my cochlea. He would have a Nucleus 24 Contour implant in the operating room in case the procedure was unsuccessful.

It didn't take me long to make my decision. I knew that if I did nothing, I would have to give up using my Nucleus 22. I had come too far in the past seven months to let that happen. Also, the thought that the receiver could break through my skin frightened me. That was not an option for me. The second option, to have a Nucleus 24 Contour implanted, was very tempting. However, if Dr. Driscoll could not insert the electrode array, I would be left without any hearing in my right ear. To me, the safest and most reasonable choice was number three.

If the repositioning surgery was unsuccessful, Dr. Driscoll would attempt to reimplant a Nucleus 24 Contour. There would be two devices in the operating room, just as there had been at my 1996 implant surgery. One, my Nucleus 22, was already in my cochlea. The other, a Nucleus 24 Contour, would be waiting in the wings, if needed. I was confident that when I woke up after surgery, one of the two would be safely tucked away in the recesses of my head. It would be the one I was meant to have.

Two weeks later, I received the information that the implant surgery would be covered by our insurance provider. I chose October 9, our son Scott's birthday, for my surgery date. Once again, I had been given the choice of sitting it out or dancing. I chose to dance. I would try again "tomorrow."

# You Still Have Your Nucleus 22

*Don't Quit*

*When things go wrong as they sometimes will.*
*When the road you're trudging is all uphill.*
*When you're feeling low and the stress is high,*
*When you want to smile but you have to sigh—*
*When worries are getting you down a bit*
*by all means pray—and don't you quit.*
*Success is failure turned inside out.*
*God's hidden gift in the clouds of doubt.*
*You never can tell how close you are.*
*It may be near when it seems so far.*
*Trust in the Lord when you're hardest hit.*
*It's when things go wrong that you must not quit.*
          —Author Unknown

At the initial activation of my Nucleus 24 Contour, the sounds I was receiving with my Nucleus 22 were not distorted and together with my Nucleus 24 Contour, I enjoyed four wonderful hours of surround sound. During the six-month period, while I was getting to know my Nucleus 24 Contour, I was waiting for the time when I could put on my Nucleus 22 and, once again be surrounded by sound. I was deeply disappointed when that day arrived and the sound was so bad. I remembered the beautiful hearing it had given me for almost five years and the four hours of surround sound after the activation of my Nucleus

24 Contour. I could have placed it in the ceramic case alongside the last hearing aid I wore and put it in my china cabinet but it was those memories that kept my journey out of silence alive. I could not quit.

So much has happened since that day. I reached the top of a hill only to be pushed back down again. Now, here I was about to climb another hill. If I reached the top again, would I remain there or would I go sliding back down again? These lines from the poem "Don't Quit" were my feelings exactly.

> You never can tell how close you are.
> It may be near when it seems so far.
> Trust in the Lord when you're hardest hit.
> It's when things go wrong that you must not quit.

I had certainly traveled far. I had a strong feeling I would reach the top. Whether I would remain there at the top or slide back down, I did not know.

Before I embarked on this journey, there was another journey for Myron and me. Remember how much I liked Colorado when I had been there in the spring of 2002? I vowed that someday I would return and Myron would come with me. Our gift from our children that Christmas was air fare to Denver. Not knowing that I would be undergoing more surgery, we made our reservations for September. Two weeks before my surgery, we flew out.

We spent a day in Colorado Springs retracing some of the steps I had taken on my first trip. We drove through the Valley of the Gods and we shopped at Old Colorado City. We drove the Pikes Peak Highway right up to the summit.

Myron enjoyed that ride very much; I did not. There were no guardrails around the many hairpin curves. Myron thought the view was breathtaking. I agreed with that! I hardly dared to

*Dora and Myron on Trailridge Road in Colorado's Rocky Mountains*

*Myron relaxing after the drive up to the summit of Pikes Peak*

breathe. I sat stone still, looking straight ahead. I thought any movement I would make could send us flying over the edge. The ride down was a bit better. At least, I dared turn my head so I could take in some views of the beautiful aspen trees that were adorned in their autumn splendor.

We spent an entire day driving on Trail Ridge Road, designated as an "All-American Road," in Rocky Mountain National Park. This was a much more enjoyable ride; there were guardrails. We stopped at many view stops along the way. The winding road took us up to 12,183 feet above sea level. When we reached the tree line, we were on the "Roof of the Rockies." There were glacier peaks wherever we looked. We could see Mt. Meeker, which is 13,911 ft.; Mt. Lady Washington at 13,281 ft.; Longs Peak, 14, 255 ft., Storm Peak, 13, 326 ft. and Pagoda Mountain at 13,497 ft. It was a breathtaking view. Carved on a marker were these words that Isabella Bird, author of *A Lady's Life in the Rocky Mountain*, used to describe the scene in 1879.

"This is a view to which nothing needs to be added.
This scenery satisfies my soul."
—*Isabella Bird*

More than a hundred years later, it was still as beautiful and it satisfied my soul. We knew we would return again but not as soon as we did. When we reached Grand Lake, we stopped for lunch, filled the gas tank and went back up. The view was every bit as beautiful the second time. We know it will be when we return again.

When we returned home, surgery was only two weeks away. While I waited, I had several chats with Pastor Strawn. Since Rochester, Minnesota is 80 miles from Spring Lake Park, I hesitated in asking him if he would drive down to give me one more prayerful sendoff to the operating room but I wanted him there. At the close of one of our visits, I asked him.

He replied, "If you want me there, I will be there."

Myron and I drove down on Wednesday, the day before my surgery. I had my pre-operative exams in the morning and visits with Dr. Driscoll and Dr. Shallop in the afternoon. My visit with Dr. Driscoll was short. When he looked at my receiver, he made the comment that my glasses were holding it up. By then, there was only room for the arm of my glasses to fit behind my ear. There was no longer room for my microphone.

My appointment with Dr. Shallop was longer. Another integrity test was needed on my Nucleus 22 so he could compare results after surgery. Once again, all tests were normal. Then, it was back to the sound treated room for more speech testing. Again, this was done so he could compare the pre-op scores to those at my activation of a Nucleus 24 Contour or the scores I would receive at the reactivation of my Nucleus 22.

My HINT sentence test scores that day were 95 percent using my Nucleus 24 Contour ESPrit 3G, 47 percent using my Nucleus 22 and using both, I scored 90 percent.

I checked into the hospital at 9 a.m. the following morning. Surgery was scheduled for 2 p.m. that afternoon. When we walked into the hospital, we found Pastor Strawn waiting for us. He accompanied us to the Outpatient Department. It was so reassuring to have him with me once again. His assurance that God would be with me during surgery was very comforting.

After I was prepped for surgery, Myron and I roamed the halls and watched television. I hadn't eaten since 8 p.m. the previous evening so by the time I went into the preinduction room, I was very hungry.

While I was waiting there, Dr. Shallop, dressed in his scrubs and wearing a Snoopy cap, came in to see how I was doing. Just having him there with his smile and cheerful manner made me feel more comfortable. He told me I could wear my Nucleus 24 Contour into the operating room. He would also see that I was wearing it when I left the room.

It was great to be able to hear the anesthesiologists and residents who came asking questions. My right ear, on which I was to have the surgery, had been marked with a black marker but still I was asked on which ear I was going to have surgery. They asked several questions about my health. I have a very healthy body. The only prescription medication I use is a nasal spray for congestion.

When I said my problems are all in my head, the nurse who was sitting by me looked up from her computer, laughed and asked, "Did I hear you right? Did you say that all your problems are in your head?"

I detected an accent when one of the residents spoke to me. When I asked where he was from, he said, "England." I said, "Of course." He was quite impressed with how well I could hear with my Nucleus 24 Contour.

As the time grew closer to going into the operating room, I became more nervous and when I get nervous, I get cold. He noticed this and went to get a preheated blanket.

Once again, I remembered the advice Pastor Galchutt had given me in 1996. "Pretend you are a little girl taking a nap for your mother." I relaxed and soon began drifting in and out of sleep.

I had a visit with one more resident. I looked down the hall and saw a tall, young man dressed in scrubs come walking toward me. He stopped by my bed, smiled, held out his hand and said, "Hello, I'm Dr. McDonald."

What a nice surprise! I knew he was practicing at Mayo but I certainly did not expect him to be part of the surgical team.

I said, "Oh, you're "Dr. McDonald's son.""

He asked if I knew his father. Yes, I certainly did. He had been my surgeon in 1985. He told me he was going to escort me into the operating room. On the ride, memories of the unsuccessful revisal stapedectomy by his father came to my mind.

I thought, *Here I am again at the Mayo Clinic for a revisal surgery. Wouldn't it be great if this time it was successful?*

I was more confident than ever that it would be successful. I also had a strong feeling that when I woke up, I would still have my Nucleus 22.

I was wide awake when I got into the operating room. Even though the mouths of the surgery team were hidden behind their masks, I had no problems conversing with them. I was waiting for the black mask to be placed over my face so I could go to sleep. When it did come, it was white and I was told to take some deep breaths. It didn't put me to sleep. A while later, it was placed there again and I heard the anesthesiologist standing behind me say, "This is oxygen. The funny stuff is in the intravenous." I fell asleep.

I woke up as I was being wheeled into the recovery room. Someone told me I still had my Nucleus 22.

I thought, *Why did he tell me that? Of course, I have my Nucleus 22!*

Then I remembered where I was. Surgery was over. After my 1996 surgery, when I was told I had a Nucleus 22 implanted, I wasn't upset. This evening when I was told I still had it, I wasn't upset. I knew that what I had was what I was meant to have.

I was wide awake when I got into recovery. I felt great. I didn't have any pain, nausea or dizziness. Best of all, I could hear. I asked the nurse what time it was. I was surprised when she said it was 6:30. At 8 p.m., I was wheeled up to my hospital room to spend the night. Myron was there waiting for me. It had been a long day for him. I told him to go to the motel and get a good night's sleep. I would see him in the morning.

# A New Home for My Nucleus 22

*"Hope is not a granted wish or a favor performed—It is a zany, unpredictable dependence on a God who loves to surprise us out of our socks."*
—Max Lucado

I did not get much sleep the nights after either my Nucleus 22 and my Nucleus 24 Contour were implanted and I did not get much sleep after my repositioning surgery. I spent a long night waiting for morning to come.

It was early when Dr. Jonathan H. Lee, the resident who assisted with the surgery, followed closely by Dr. Shallop, came to my room to remove my turban and discuss my surgery with me. Both were a bit apologetic that I was not reimplanted with the Nucleus 24 Contour. I assured them I was happy to have had a skilled surgeon and was not disappointed. I was confident I had what I was meant to have.

Dr. Driscoll came to my room shortly after they left. He, too, seemed to think I had my heart set on being reimplanted with the Nucleus 24 Contour. I told him I was not disappointed and had faith that when it was reactivated, the harsh, rumbly sound would be gone. I was told to return for follow-up with him and with Dr. Shallop on October 30. He told me I did not have to wait until then to find out if the surgery had solved my problem. I could begin to use my Nucleus 22 in two weeks or when the swelling had gone down. I assured him I would wait until the 30th.

I was determined to wait but my natural curiosity got the best of me. I didn't even listen to Dr. Driscoll's recommendation that I wait for two weeks. My incision healed rapidly and soon I was searching for the receiver. Once I found it, there was no holding me back. It was constantly on my mind.

One afternoon, when I was on my computer, I got up and went into the kitchen. I took the Nucleus 22 processor out of the Dry Aid Kit, disconnected the lapel microphone from the processor and reconnected the microphone earpiece. I didn't put it on my ear that day; I waited until the next morning when Myron was home. I wanted to share my joy with him. Yes, I was confident that the sound had changed. How much it had changed was a surprise and, yes, it surprised me out of my socks.

While Myron was still in bed, I went into the kitchen. I sat down by the table, took my Nucleus 22 processor out of the Dry Aid Kit and placed a battery in it. It took awhile for me to find the internal magnet as I was still looking for it to be in its old home. Finally, I remembered that it had moved over toward the back of my head. The two magnets grasped and I turned on the processor.

I was awe struck! For the first time ever with my Nucleus 22, I heard the bird clock tick! Myron came around the corner. He didn't know what I was up to as we greeted each other. It took some time before I realized that his voice sounded so natural. When I told him I had only my Nucleus 22 on, he didn't believe me until I showed him. Then, he went into the bathroom to get ready for work. When I passed the bathroom, I could hear the water running in the shower. I went into the kitchen and I could hear the hair dryer from around the corner.

After Myron went to work, I e-mailed Dr. Shallop and told him the good news. He, in turn, told Dr. Driscoll and then he e-mailed me back, saying how happy they were for me. I couldn't wait to see them and prove just how well I could hear with my

Nucleus 22. I also wanted to thank them for what they had done for me.

Since Myron had taken off so many days from work, he felt I should go alone for my appointment. He had confidence that, with two good ears, I would be able to fend for myself. He drove me down early in the morning and dropped me off in front of the Mayo Building. He wished me luck and said he would see me Friday evening. My appointment with Dr. Shallop was at 9 a.m. and I made it without a minute to spare.

We went right to work. Since I had not been wearing my Nucleus 22 for two weeks, Dr. Shallop thought he should recheck my comfort and threshold levels once again. That done, he left the room and returned with two Nucleus 22 processors.

He said, "I am going to give you three programs to experiment with while you are waiting for your appointment tomorrow afternoon."

Then, he placed tape on the processors and marked each one. Number 107 was the MAP I had on my processor when I came in that morning. Numbers 108 and 109 were new MAPS. I was then off for my appointment with Dr. Driscoll.

Dr. Driscoll was very happy with the results of the repositioning surgery. He told me surgery had been carried out without complications and the device was functioning when Dr. Shallop tested it. He also told me the incision had healed nicely. I assured him I was satisfied with the results. There was one thing I needed to know. I asked him if the time should come when I could not use my Nucleus 22, if he could reimplant a Nucleus 24 Contour.

He smiled and answered, "Sure, I could even implant a Nucleus 30 Contour."

It was then time to begin my experiments with the three different MAPS. I had lunch in the Mayo Visitor Cafeteria. On the way out, I sat down by the waterfall near the entrance of the cafeteria.

*Dora with her surgeon, Dr. Collin L.W. Driscoll.*

First, I listened with MAP Number 107, the MAP I was using when I left Dr. Shallop's office. It sounded like a waterfall should sound.

Since I didn't have three microphones, I had to unplug the microphone and then plug it into the next processor. I found that MAP Number 109 sounded rough; program MAP Number 108 sounded high pitched.

I went through the procedure again while listening to the piano. When I listened with MAP Number 109, there was a great deal of banging and clashing. I heard the low keys with MAP Number 107. By the time I had the microphone plugged into the processor that held MAP Number 108, the pianist had quit playing.

Then, I went into a smaller cafeteria for coffee. Using MAP Number 109, the ventilation system as well as the voices of patrons sounded rough. The ventilation system remained rough sounding and the words of the patrons were indistinguishable while using MAP Number 108. With MAP Number 107, the voices remained indistinguishable but the ventilation system was quieter. Before I left for my motel, I went back to check the piano. MAPS Number 107 and Number 109 sounded okay. Now there was a lot of clashing and banging with MAP Number 108. It seemed as though I wasn't getting anywhere with my experiments. It was time to go to my motel and sleep on it. I would do some more listening in the morning.

When I awoke, I set to work. I turned TV to the weather channel. With MAP Number 107, the weatherman's words were indistinguishable. The only words I picked out were "temperature" and "tonight." With MAP Number 108, I could understand full sentences. There was a loud pitch whine along with his voice. His voice was rough sounding when I switched to MAP Number 109 but I was able to understand more words. "Minnesota, Wisconsin and Iowa" were added to the list of words that I understood.

Then, I switched to Channel 5 News. I understood much of what was said with MAP Number 108 but words were indistinguishable using MAP Numbers 107 and 109. My own voice sounded best with MAP Number 109. Water running was high pitched with MAP Number 107 and normal sounding with Numbers 107 and 109. Pulling drawers open and switching the light switch on and off sounded normal with all three MAPS. It was then time to leave for the Mayo Building.

While having breakfast in the cafeteria, I switched between the three processors. The voices of several ladies sitting at a table near me were squished, rumbly and indistinguishable with all three MAPS. There was a rack for dirty dishes nearby. When I used MAPS Numbers 109 and 107, the dishes banged squeakily. They banged clearly with MAP Number 108.

I experimented using my Nucleus 24 Contour with each processor. The voices of the ladies remained squished and I could not distinguish them. The banging of the dishes was loud but sounded like dishes sound when they bang up against the other while using MAPS Numbers 107 and 108. With MAP Number 109, the sound was squeaky. It was time to bring the results of my experiments to show Dr. Shallop.

He looked over my notes and quickly eliminated MAP Number 109. I returned to the sound treated room for speech testing using MAP Numbers 107 and 108. With MAP Number 107, I scored 25 percent and with MAP Number 108, I scored 46 percent. He sent me home with MAP Number 107 on one Nucleus 22 processor and MAP Number 108 on another. He did not tell me which was which. He told me to choose which MAP I liked the best and to return later. I was using MAP Number 108 when I left his office and continued with it for several days. Once again, I kept a journal.

*My Journal*

**Sunday, November 2**—Myron and I went to church today. We sat in the back so it was difficult to hear the sermon. I did manage to pick up some of the words and a few sentences. The music sounded very good and I followed along easily with the liturgy.

I used only my Nucleus 22 most of the afternoon. Listening to my CDs, some sounded good and others not so good. Myron's voice is improving. He is running out of patience with me, though. I can't blame him as for the past two years all I have been doing is getting used to a different strategy or MAP. He knows I can hear so well with my Nucleus 24 Contour ESPrit 3G and can't figure out why I don't just use that. Guess he doesn't know that I love my Nucleus 22 too much and that I like a challenge.

**Monday, November 3**—I walked to McDonald's this morning. The piped in music sounded really good; the lyrics are just in reach.

I can hear the "beep, beep, beep" of the hash brown deep fryer clearly over the music.

Tuesday, November 4—The sound of newspapers and running water are again uncomfortable but I don't mind as I know the sounds will improve. While I was frying hamburger, it reminded me of frying bacon the first day my Nucleus 22 was activated. There were a lot of snapping and crackling sounds.

Wednesday, November 5—I am catching the phrases on TV with the use of closed captioning but the two processors don't seem to be meshing like they had done in the past. My Nucleus 22 seems to be the dominant processor right now.

Thursday, November 6—I listened to my Johnny Cash CD before I went for a walk. He sounded okay. I had breakfast at McDonald's. The music this morning was so squeaky, it made my head whirl. Something strange is going on.

Friday, November 7—I put my Nucleus 24 Contour ESPrit 3G on and listened with it alone for awhile. Everything sounded very good. Then, I added my Nucleus 22. Sounds turned very bad. I listened to my Tennessee Ernie Ford CD. All the words were in-distinguishable. I turned on TV and that also sounded bad.

Saturday, November 8—Again, I listened to Tennessee Ernie Ford. He continued to sound bad. This made me very frustrated. I thought I would see what MAP Number 107 sounded like so I switched processors. The sound improved immediately. I listened to Tennessee Ernie Ford again and the lyrics came through very clearly. I turned TV on and was able to understand much of what was said.

Monday, November 10—I began to wonder, since it was Halloween when Dr. Shallop had mapped me, did he trick me and switch the numbers of my processors? I e-mailed him to find out and he e-mailed me back, "NO TRICKS!"

Tuesday, November 11—I am now using MAP Number 107. I check out MAP Number 108 occasionally. It makes my head whirl and sounds are very jumpy.

Wednesday, November 12—MAP Number 107 is coming along nicely. Myron and I had a conversation without any problems. He was surprised when I told him I had only my Nucleus 22 on.

Thursday, November 13—I felt very brave today. I started out the day using only my Nucleus 22. I played Monopoly with my grandsons, Jeffery and Justin, before they left for school. I didn't have any trouble understanding them. My CDs sound great with my Nucleus 22 alone and with my Nucleus 24 Contour ESPrit 3G alone but they sound the best when I have both on.

Friday, November 14—Again, I started the day with only my Nucleus 22. While I was sitting by the window in the living room waiting for Jeffery and Justin to wake up, I could hear the birds chirping, our neighbor dog barking and cars going past.

My last entry was:

Saturday, November 15—My hearing with my Nucleus 22, since my repositioning, is far better than I had ever dreamed. I am beginning to think it is superior to my Nucleus 24 Contour ESPrit 3G with environmental sounds. Speech is clearer with my Nucleus 24 Contour ESPrit 3G; the two together make for wonderful hearing. One thing that disappoints me is that the telephone is still not clear to me when I use my Nucleus 22. Other than that, I don't think my hearing could get any better.

When I began to write this book, *I Danced: A Cochlear Implant Odyssey,* it was my intention to share my experience with my sequential bilateral Nucleus 22 and Nucleus 24 Contour cochlear implants. It was my hope that by sharing my experiences with variable mode mapping, readers facing difficulties with their implants would be inspired and not give up.

I did not know, then, that I would be facing an even greater decision when my receiver migrated and I had to choose between a reimplantation or a repositioning of my receiver.

One morning this spring, while reading the morning newspaper, I came across this saying written by Dan Zadra, "Have faith—things fall apart so that they can fall together." I thought how relevant it is to my story.

*I Danced: A Cochlear Implant Odyssey* should have ended here but there was one more surprise waiting for me just up the road. I was going to receive my Nucleus 22 ESPrit 3G.

# Cochlear Implant Integrity Test

*by John K. Shallop, Ph.D.*

P resent day cochlear implants (CI) sometimes require special testing to determine if the internal implant components are functioning correctly. These components include the receiving antenna (coil), integrated computer 'chip' and the electrode array. The implant chip is the heart of all modern cochlear implants. It receives instruction signals continuously from the external speech processor by forward radio frequency telemetry when the speech processor is turned on. Some cochlear implants can also send information back to the speech processor by radio frequency telemetry. The electrode array includes the insulated wires connected to the implanted chip and the multiple 'active' electrodes in the cochlea and the ground electrodes(s). Now let's look at how a CI can be tested objectively in combination with patient comments and reports.

Suppose an adult CI patient reports "the quality of speech is suddenly getting worse" or the parents of a CI child say "our child has suddenly shown a lack of response to sound after doing so well." First of all, we will assume that your audiologist has checked all of the external components: the speech processor, batteries, cables and coil. If these components are all okay, then we will proceed with objective integrity testing. Both of these examples are clear indications for integrity testing of the CI. So, let us consider how to 'test' the functioning of the internal components of a cochlear implant.

Our first test will be to evaluate the function of all active and ground electrodes. The programming software usually enables us to quickly check each of the active and ground electrodes by measuring the electrical resistance (impedance) of each electrode in 'ohms.' This value is typically in the range of 1000 to 10,000 ohms. If electrodes are abnormal, these impedance values are very low (for example, 100 ohms) on two electrodes such as electrodes 2 and 11, this result suggests that these electrodes are shorted to each other. When electrodes are shorted together, they no longer produce signals, which are heard as two different pitches. Rather, when these two electrodes are stimulated alone, they both produce a signal that the patient hears as the same pitch, typically midway between the individual electrodes. There can still be a distinct perception of pitch when two electrodes are shorted but the perceived pitch will be the same for both electrodes.

Another possible finding for the electrode test includes an open circuit. In this case the electrode is not able to produce any neural stimulation because current from the CI chip does not get to the electrode because of the open circuit. An example of an open circuit would include a broken electrode wire. In such cases the open circuit electrode would be turned off in the patient's program 'map.'

There are a series of tests that we can conduct to see if the patient's CI is functioning normally after the electrodes have been tested. These tests vary depending on the specific brand and CI model. Small disk electrodes can be placed on the patient's head to measure voltage signals for small stimulation current for each electrode. These measures are called surface voltages and they are simple to obtain, but they require experience to interpret. The patterns of these surface voltages can reveal problems with the CI or changes in the patient's cochlear anatomy. Some CI devices also have the ability to use "back" telemetry to measure various technical functions. These tests are usually done with special software provided by the CI company at the request of your CI audiologist. It has become more common for modern cochlear implants to be able to measure the responses of the hearing nerve directly through the implant. These nerve response measurements can be helpful in deciding whether a cochlear implant is producing effective stimulation of the hearing nerve.

CI patients should always inform their audiologist whenever they notice sudden changes in their hearing or if they notice any unusual sensations while using their cochlear implant. If problems cannot be resolved through normal programming, then an integrity test may be indicated.

> Jon K. Shallop, Ph.D.
> Associate Professor of Audiology
> Mayo Medical School
> Rochester, Minnesota

"Have faith—Things fall apart so
that things can fall together."
—Dan Zadra

# Part Four

# Reflections and Recollections
## 2004

I knew the Nucleus 22 ESPrit 3G, the behind-the-ear processor that is compatible with the Nucleus 22 cochlear implant, was going to be the same size as that of the Nucleus 24 Contour ESPrit 3G. In anticipation of receiving one, often I would put on my Nucleus 24 Contour 3G behind the ear on which rested the microphone of my Nucleus 22 Body Worn Processor (BWP).

When the receiver of my Nucleus 22 migrated, the processor no longer fit behind my ear so I reconciled myself to always wearing my BWP. With the repositioning of the receiver, a new home was prepared for my Nucleus 22 ESPrit 3G. When I read Dan Zadra's quote, I realized just how relevant it is to my odyssey. All the while, God had been charting a safe course for me.

# A Course Well Charted

*"We do not understand the intricate pattern of the stars in their courses but we know He who created them does, and that surely as He guides them He is charting a safe course for us."*

—Billy Graham

On Friday, February 6, at 7 a.m., Myron and I were on the road to Rochester, Minnesota. My appointment with Dr. Shallop to program my Nucleus 22 ESPrit 3G, was at 9:30 a.m. Southern Minnesota was to have received eight inches of snow overnight. Myron is very cautious about driving in bad weather so I expected him to tell me we would stay home but he was as excited as I was. Wild Horses could not have keep us from going.

The roads were in good driving condition until we were about 15 miles from Rochester. Then, they turned icy. We passed several cars that had slid off the road and were sitting in the ditch. An ambulance came up from behind and passed us. A few miles up the road we came upon an accident. A van had slid down a steep ravine and flipped over. There were several ambulances and police cars there. Myron had been driving slowly but he slowed down even more. We crept the rest of the way into the city. Even so, we were only a few minutes late arriving for my appointment.

We found Dr. Shallop standing outside his office, waiting for me. He smiled when we walked in, pointed to his desk and said, "We have everything ready for you."

Just then, several audiologists came out of an adjacent office.

*Dora describes the sound she hears with her Nucleus 22 ESPrit 3G*

He explained, "We are going to have a lot of company today. They want to watch the activation of the first Nucleus 22 ESPrit 3G."

I had gone through the activations of my Nucleus 22, my Nucleus 24 Contour, my Nucleus 24 Contour 3G and the reactivation of my Nucleus 22 after my repositioning surgery. I can say, without a doubt, that the activation of my Nucleus 22 ESPrit 3G made me the most nervous of all. When I conveyed my nervousness to Dr. Shallop, he asked me, "Why?"

I answered, "Because I want so much for it to work!"

He replied, "It will."

Dr. Shallop's plan was to unload the MAP of my Nucleus 22 body worn processor into the processor of the Nucleus 22 ESPrit 3G but he ran into problems. The software would not accept all aspects of my variable mode MAP. He did some tinkering and then we proceeded to go through the process of finding my threshold and comfort levels. As I listened to the beeps of my electrodes, I began to relax and a smile came to my face. They all had such a beautiful ring to them and none caused facial stimulation. We went through the process of balancing the loudness of my electrodes; a few adjustments needed to be done. That done, it was time for the "sweep" of all the electrodes. An even bigger smile came to my face. It sounded like I was listening to the keys of a well-tuned piano.

Dr. Shallop turned on the switch of the processor and said, "Hello, are you there?"

I heard his voice clearly but I also heard something else. It reminded me of the sound I heard prior to having my Nucleus 22 receiver repositioned. When I told him this, he thought for a minute and then said that I might be hearing the fan on his computer.

He did some more adjusting to it and when my processor was turned on again, that sound was gone. Dr. Shallop's voice, Myron's voice and the voices of each of the audiologists sounded so nice.

By then, we were all ready for a break. Dr. Shallop told me to have coffee and check out the sounds outside his office. My friend, Bev, who had come to join us, accompanied Myron and me to Starbucks. The noise of coffee brewers was very loud so I turned the sensitivity down on both processors. I didn't have any problems conversing there or later when we had lunch at a busy restaurant.

After we finished lunch, Myron and I returned to the clinic where I was to have more programming and undergo speech testing. Volume with auto-sensitivity, which would automatically lower unusually loud sounds, was put in slot Number Two of my processor. Then, it was off to the sound-treated room for speech testing. My hearing-in-noise test (HINT) sentence scores with my Nucleus 24 Contour ESPrit 3G were 88 and 96 percent. With both my Nucleus 22 ESPrit 3G and Nucleus 24 Contour ESPrit

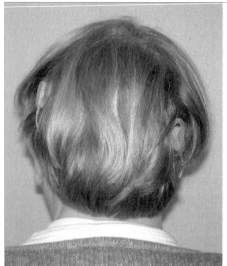

*Dora's "Twins"—her nucleus 22 and N24 Contour Esprit 3G's (notice the difference in position of her transmitters). Right: Dora's smile shows her happiness.*

3G, my scores were 97 and 100 percent. I was very apprehensive when the testing with my Nucleus 22 ESPrit 3G began and I got a slow start. I missed the first two sentences but I recovered well with the remaining sentences. My scores were 77 and 78 percent. It was those scores that interested everyone.

I also did some directionality testing and was encircled by eight speakers.

As Dr. Shallop asked me, "Where is my voice?" I was to tell him from which speaker I heard his voice.

I scored exceptionally well when tested using both processors. As with previous testing when I had only my Nucleus 22 BWP or my Nucleus 24 Contour ESPrit 3G on, I was not able to tell which speaker his voice was at. It was always on the side of the processor I was using. After I finished the testing, it was 3:30 p.m. and time to head for home. Dr. Shallop, Myron and I ended the session feeling very gratified.

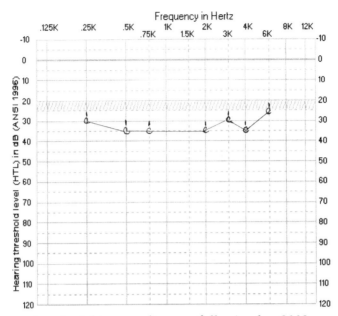

*Dora's right ear audiogram following her 2003 repositioning surgery of her Nucleus 22 implant*

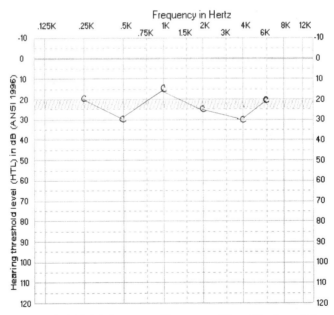

*Dora's 2004 left ear audiogram of her Nucleus 24 Contour cochlear implant system*

On the drive home, I became very disappointed. I put a John Phillip Sousa CD in our car's CD player and sat back to listen. I could not hear the music with my Nucleus 22 ESPrit 3G. Switching from sensitivity to volume and having it as loud as it would go, did not help. I finally gave up and listened with my Nucleus 24 Contour ESPrit 3G. I was very worried!

The first thing I did when I arrived home was to hurry into the den and put the Jim Reeves CD, that I used as a tester, on my boombox. I turned my Nucleus 24 Contour ESPrit 3G off and set the sensitivity of my Nucleus 22 ESPrit 3G on Number Four. I heard, "Put your sweet lips a little closer to the phone," come through loud and clear. Then I sat back and listened. I also tried the volume setting and that, too, sounded very nice.

Patti Page and Doris Day had not sounded good since I began having problems with my Nucleus 22. I thought I would check them out. Patti Page sang "Tennessee Waltz" beautifully. I fast forwarded to "Mockingbird Hill." The words "Tra la la, Tweedle dee dee dee, It gives me a thrill, To wake up in the morning, To the mockingbird's trill" was so pretty. I played it over and over.

# Sweet Sounds

*"Hope is the thing with feathers—*
*that perches in the soul*
*and sings the tune without the words—*
*and never stops at all."*
—Emily Dickinson

*My Journal*

**Saturday, February 7**—This morning when I got up, I didn't hesitate to put my Nucleus 22 ESPrit 3G on first. I set it on my volume program and turned the dial up until I could hear the ticking of our bird clock. I checked to see what the setting was and it was on Number Four. I went down to check my e-mails and answered a few. The clicking of the keyboard and the computer fan sounded very much like I hear them with my Nucleus 24 Contour ESPrit 3G. I heard the sound of the furnace kicking in and the air blowing through the vent. All these sounds are so very pleasant.

I went upstairs to make breakfast. The snapping and crackling of my frying egg, the toast popping up out of the toaster, the bubbling of the oatmeal as it cooked, the whirring of the microwave and even the banging and clanging of the dishes and the silver sounded pleasant to my ears. When I turned the water faucet on, it sounded very shrill and loud. I was surprised and, yes, I became worried when suddenly the volume dropped. I turned the dial up to Number Five and the sound did not get louder.

It took a while for me to remember that I had auto sensitivity programmed into my volume setting. When I turned the faucet off, the sounds began to get normal. I thought back to the drive home from the cochlear implant facility last night and thought,

*Aha! That is why the music wasn't loud enough.* The music plus the sounds of the road caused the autosensitivity to kick in. I don't think I am going to like auto sensitivity. I like hearing everything and I like being in control and loud sounds don't bother me a bit.

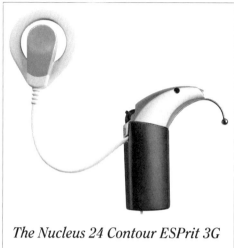

*The Nucleus 24 Contour ESPrit 3G*

After breakfast, I went into the living room to relax over a cup of coffee. I heard a very faint, high-pitched sound. I thought I may be hearing the sparrows out in the evergreen by the window. When I saw our drapes blowing, I realized the furnace had come on and the sound was the air blowing through the vent. Myron got up and it was easy to converse with him. When he went into the bathroom, I could hear the whirring of the hair dryer through the closed bathroom door.

Myron and I planned to go to the mall and walk but before we did, I went out to shovel the snow we had received over night. Always before, the scraping of the shovel on the pavement had been so screechy. This morning, the sound was quite pleasant. Then, I knew why Myron never complained about the sound. I had not been hearing it like he did.

Before we left for the mall, I put my Nucleus 24 Contour ESPrit 3G on. It was like putting on my Nucleus 22 ESPrit 3G. The sounds are so similar and the two processors blend beautifully. I gave them a nickname. I call them "my twins born 21 months apart."

The first thing I noticed when I walked into the mall was that the piped in music sounded so much clearer. I still could not recognize the lyrics but the instrumental part sounded so pleasant. The noise was not nearly as loud in the corridors. When I ordered a pretzel at Aunt Martha's, I heard the cashier ask me, "How are you today?"

I think I must have been smiling. When I met people they looked at me and smiled. Do you suppose the cloud I was floating on was not invisible after all?

It was a busy day today. We went to our grandson Jacob's hockey game this afternoon. Instead of going into the arena, we sat by a table near a big window in full view of the rink. There were many fans roaming around. It had always been so noisy for me but today I didn't even think about the noise. I was able to visit easily with my family. Jacob's team lost 10 to 1.

The day was not yet over. From the ice arena, we went to Prince of Peace Church to attend a farewell party for our neighbor's son and his family who are moving to Georgia. On the drive over, Myron said it would be the ultimate test for me. The acoustics of the room are so bad that hearing-impaired parishioners shun the room. I passed the test with flying colors. There was a good turnout and it got loud but I had no problem conversing with anyone.

**Sunday, February 8**—Again, I put my Nucleus 22 ESPrit 3G on first this morning. The microwave is louder today but the beeps at the end of the cycle are little baby beeps. Again, the sounds of making breakfast were so nice. After breakfast, I retired to the living room to listen to a Tennessee Ernie Ford CD while I enjoyed my morning coffee. His voice is very high-pitched today but I do understand the lyrics clearly. I noticed that every once in a while, the volume goes way down. Must be the autosensitivity kicking in. I do not like it. I will have to talk to Dr. Shallop about that at my next appointment. I switched to sensitivity and it solved the problem but I don't like the sound as well as I do with volume.

Our grandson, Jeffery, wanted grandpa and me to come to his basketball tournament today so we didn't go to church. The games were played in a huge dome with four games going on at the same time. I heard the whistles of the referees and the buzzers going off constantly. I had been there before and the noise was almost unbearable. Today, it didn't bother me. I think the auto sensitivity kicked in. It is great for circumstances like this.

Monday, February 8—Again, I started the day wearing my Nucleus 22 ESPrit 3G. I wanted to see if I could understand my grandsons, Jeffery and Justin. I didn't have too great a difficulty but I did need quite a few repeats. After they left for school, I listened to Tennessee Ernie Ford again. His voice was not quite as high pitched. The word "sweet" in the song, "Sweet Hour of Prayer" and the word "sheaves" in "Bringing in the Sheaves" are extremely shrill.

I called Myron this morning using my telecoil. His voice needed more volume but I did understand every word he said. This is the first time I had called him using my Nucleus 22 for over two years.

I was home alone today with only the sounds of the house to hear. I listened to CDs and I spent some time watching television. I understood voices clearly as I followed along with closed captioning. I hear some voices without the use of closed captioning.

Tuesday, February 9—This morning it was easier understanding my grandsons. I even forgot that I didn't have my Nucleus 24 Contour ESPrit 3G on. The telephone rang while I was eating breakfast. When I checked our caller ID, I saw that it was my neighbor, Pat. Without hesitating, I lifted the receiver and said, "Hello." I heard Pat say, "Hello, Dora, how are you?"

Her voice was faint but very clear. We talked for awhile but then I told her I would call her back on my tele-coil adaptable phone. Instead of just switching the telecoil of my Nucleus 22 ESPrit 3G on, I put on my Nucleus 24 Contour ESPrit 3G. I guess the kitchen telephone is my Nucleus 22 telephone and the telephone in my den is for my Nucleus 24 Contour.

I listened to Tennessee Ernie Ford again. His voice is getting closer to normal. The word "sweet" is still high-pitched. I think I detect a woman's voice in the accompanying choir. I called Myron and, this time, his voice was louder.

Wednesday, February 10—I played Battleship with my grandsons before they went off to school this morning. It is very interesting listening to the letters and numbers as they call them, trying to sink each other's ships. I heard maybe half of them correctly.

Tennessee Ernie Ford's voice sounds better.

I went out with my neighbor friends for lunch today. I didn't have any problems in placing my order or in following the fast and changing conversation. I sense that they are no longer as watchful of me. I wore both processors.

I watched "60 Minutes" this evening with just my Nucleus 22 ESPrit 3G. I heard quite well without closed captioning.

Thursday, February 11—I played Battleship with Jeffery and Justin again this morning. The letters and numbers were easier to understand.

I called Myron and used sensitivity this time; his voice was easier to understand. Tennessee Ernie Ford's voice is still high pitched but is getting better. The "E" sounds are still quite shrill. Television is improving. The voices of men are better than womens' voices.

Friday, February 12—I put on both processors and went to the mall to spend the day. I had breakfast at McDonald's and soaked up all the sounds. Every Friday, a large group of senior citizens meets there for breakfast. The noise generated by the group had always bothered me before but because they so obviously enjoy the company of one another, I tried to block it out. Today the conversations and laughter are much mellower. I actually am able to understand some of the comments that are shared. The sound in the mall was more mellow, also. I had lunch at Arby's Restaurant. A little boy, about two years old, and his mom were sitting in the booth in front of me. When they were getting ready to leave, the little boy turned around. When he saw me, he smiled and said, "Oh, Grandma!"

His mother started to apologize but I interrupted her. I told her I have six grandchildren but I would be happy to have him, too! It is just so much fun to be able to hear all these wonderful things.

Myron and I drove out to his hometown, Chaska, this evening to take in a Hawks basketball game. The high school team is rated #1 in the state of Minnesota so there was a huge crowd there. I didn't notice a reduced rate for senior citizen tickets so I asked the cashier. He waved us right through. We did stop and tell them that Myron had graduated from the high school. The pep band sounded great but, as the gym filled up, the noise increased. I turned the sensitivity of both processors down as far as they could go and I could still hear very well. Myron and I conversed easily on the drive home.

# Reflecting, Recollecting, Relaxing

*"The greater the happiness, the greater could be the sadness. The more exciting the achievement, the more devastating could be the failure. These are the chances we take when we reach for something worthwhile."*

—Freddie Mitman

I heard the Bell Choir when they played on Easter Sunday. When Myron and I arrived for the service that morning, we found the pews up front already occupied so we had to sit at the back. When I opened the bulletin and read that the Bell Choir would be playing before the service began, I didn't hesitate for a minute. I leaned over and told Myron I was going out to the Narthex so I could hear them. I did not recognize the song they were playing but that did not matter. The bells were clear and true.

After a long, cold winter, the song birds are again singing merrily here in Minnesota. I can recognize the refrains of the cardinals, robins, wrens, doves, finches and sparrows which have become inscribed in my memory, but there are some songs I have forgotten over the winter. One day, when I was out for my walk, I heard a rapid twittering over and over. Last spring it would have bothered me when I did not know which bird was singing. That doesn't bother me anymore. I have learned to relax and just enjoy the singing.

My perennials are coming up in my flower beds. Like the birds, I recognize those that are most familiar to me—the mums, day lilies, hosta and iris. Over the winter, I forgot the names of many others. Last spring it would have bothered me and I would have asked my friend, Barb, for help. It doesn't bother me anymore. I have learned to relax and enjoy their beauty.

When I listen to symphonies on our stereo, I can differentiate between the different musical instruments. For a long time, it was very distressing when I did not know the names of the instruments. This doesn't bother me anymore. I have learned to relax and enjoy the beautiful music.

For the past year, my Nucleus 22 cochlear implant has been receiving much more attention than my Nucleus 24 Contour. Despite Dr. Shallop's recommendation that I wear both processors at all times, I concentrated on wearing only my Nucleus 22 ESPrit 3G. Recently, that changed when I attended a reception for Miss America 1995, Heather Whitestone McCallum. It was noisy in the reception hall but I didn't have any problems understanding anyone.

I did some experimenting while I was there. First, I held the magnet of my Nucleus 22 ESPrit 3G away from my head. All sound moved over on the side of my Nucleus 24 Contour ESPrit 3G. I did the same with my Nucleus 24 Contour ESPrit 3G. Everyone had moved to the side of my Nucleus 22 ESPrit 3G. Since that evening, I have started each day wearing both my processors and I leave them on until I retire for the night. I have learned to relax and enjoy the wonderful surround sound that my sequential bilateral implants give me.

When I began to write this book, it was my intention to share my experiences of bilateral hearing, the regaining of my hearing with my Nucleus 22 with variable mode programming and the importance of never giving up. I did not contemplate any more changes.

Nine months later, I experienced another setback. The receiv-

*The Nucleus 24 Contour ESPrit 3G and the Nucleus 22 Contour ESPrit 3G. Dora found that when placed together, they (appropriately) form a heart.*

er of my Nucleus 22 migrated and I needed to make a decision. If there was any chance of regaining the wonderful hearing I had once experienced, I would have to undergo another ear surgery. I had achieved very much since my Nucleus 22 was implanted in 1996, so I was well aware that a failure would be very disappointing. I knew I could not sit it out; I would dance once more.

The morning after my repositioning surgery, I was very tired both mentally and physically. When Myron came to the hospital that morning, I told him I would not go through another ear surgery. A month later, when my Nucleus 22 was reactivated and I could hear so much better, I changed my mind. In February, when I received my Nucleus 22 ESPrit 3G and my hearing improved even more, I reaffirmed that decision.

I do not know if the hearing I am now receiving with my Nucleus 24 Contour ESPrit 3G and my Nucleus 22 ESPrit 3G will have a lasting success. I do not know if I am being granted another respite in my journey before another obstacle is placed in my path. I do know that, should this happen, my hearing is too precious for me to not try one more time. I will take one more leap of faith. If I am given the choice of sitting it out or dancing, I will choose to dance. It is my wish that you will dance along with me,

I have left a comma and not ended my story with a period. My journey continues and, if you or someone you know, could benefit from a cochlear implant, I hope you will seek all the assistance that is out there waiting for you.

*"Hope, like love, transcends all time.*
*It is the song inside the heart that never stops singing.*
*To see our journey through the eyes of hope is to know*
*that all is happening as it was meant to."*
*—Flavia*

# Finding Help for Your Hearing Loss

*by Terry D. Portis, Ed.D.*
*Executive Director of Self Help for Hearing Loss (SHHH)*

One of the most puzzling problems I have encountered in my work with people who have a hearing loss is a reluctance to seek out any help at all.

Looking at the statistics, we know that most of the 26 million people who have a hearing loss will never do anything about it. About five million will do something about their hearing loss, but most of these folks will take action only after someone close to them has encouraged them to seek help.

Why is it so hard for a person to first admit they are starting to lose their hearing, and then to do something about it? I have thought about this many times and come up with some ideas. In this chapter, I would like to discuss why people are reluctant to seek help, the kinds of help that are available, and conclude with some thoughts on what a difference help can make in a person's life.

## Why don't people seek help for their hearing loss?

*It does not affect my life.*

Once when I was in Sarasota, Florida, I was enjoying a beautiful late afternoon on the beach. I was floating in the Gulf of Mexico, really enjoying myself. To me, this is what vacation is supposed to be about!

Off in the distance I heard my wife calling to me, which woke me up! I had drifted off to sleep and drifted away from shore.

The water was very clear and I could see the sandy gulf bottom, about 20 feet below me. This is not a problem if you can swim, but I cannot. (The fact of my not swimming is a source of family shame for my dad, the Navy veteran and expert swimmer). I began to kick with all my might, but the tide was pulling me out. My wife and children were screaming at me to kick harder, but it was not doing any good. Not only was I in over my head, I am sure I looked like a big seal to any passing sharks in the area. My situation was pretty bleak and getting worse.

A solitary early evening swimmer "happened" to be swimming by. He casually asked me if I needed help and I calmly answered that I did. He grabbed the rope of my float and pulled me to shore, where my wife and kids were both happy to see me alive and angry at me for getting myself into this mess. It certainly was not my time to go.

If you are experiencing a hearing loss, you are a lot like me on the raft. There is a pull on you, an undercurrent towards isolation. Maybe you are asleep when it starts to happen and you are drifting away from shore without realizing it. You may be telling yourself that your hearing loss is not really affecting your life.

At first you stopped going to parties, then you stopped going to the movies, then you stopped talking on the phone and one day you stopped going to church. Before you knew it, you were isolated and lonely. Like me on the raft, you may have heard people calling for you to come back to shore, but you either did not listen or felt powerless to do anything about it. If this describes you, do not beat yourself up for finding yourself isolated and alone. This is what hearing loss does to you.

*People will not understand.*

If you fell and broke your leg today, everyone around you would understand what this meant for you. They would know you were headed to the hospital, that you were going to need rehabilitation, that once you got walking again you would be walking with a limp for a while. So, knowing that people will understand, and sympathize, you would not hesitate to let people know what had happened to you.

Hearing loss, though, seems different than something like a broken leg, or even a bad back. Why do you seem to hear better than at other times? Why can you understand some people when they talk better than others? You have a hearing aid now, so why are you still having trouble hearing? You decide it is not worth the trouble, and so you hide it, or fake it.

*You would have to admit the problem.*

Sometimes a decision to get some help means a decision to admit that a problem has gotten pretty bad. It is hard to admit to oneself and others that your hearing has deteriorated to the point that it is really affecting your life. Many people may go a long time by saying, "It's really not that bad."

Other people around you, if they were honest, would tell you differently. They would tell you that when they were in the car with you, you did not hear the siren of an oncoming fire truck. They would tell you that the TV is so loud they dread watching it with you. They would tell you that they can tell you are not hearing people when they talk. They know you have a problem with your hearing, even if you do not know yourself.

## What kind of help is available?

Once people decide to get help, what kind of help should they get? Where do they go, who do they talk to?

*Technological Help*

The first kind of help is technological. There have been so many advances in hearing assistive technology in recent years and people are able to benefit like never before. Your first step is to visit your family doctor and make sure there is not some medical reason for your hearing loss. For most people, their hearing loss is the result of too much noise or just heredity. Your second step is to visit an audiologist who can test your hearing and recommend a hearing aid. If your hearing loss is severe enough, you may be a candidate for a cochlear implant.

Beyond the hearing aid, there are other types of hearing assistive technology that may help you. I recommend you visit the National Center for Hearing Assistive Technology website to find out what is available. The address is *www.hearingloss.org/hat*. My wife, who has a hearing loss, has benefited from a device that helps her hear me when we are at a restaurant. She also has a personal TV loop pad that lets her hear the TV like she has not for years. Do not be intimidated by these devices. Educate yourself and see what is available.

*Self Help*

Because I am the executive director of Self Help for Hard of Hearing People, it is not surprising that I am talking about self help. Self help means two things: first, you inform yourself and secondly, you stand up for yourself.

By informing yourself, you become something of an expert on your own hearing loss. You learn how others have managed their problems with hearing, the strategies they have used, and then make them your own. An old cliché states that knowledge is power, but it is really true with hearing loss. Knowledge gives you the power to take charge of your own hearing, and how you are going to deal with it. There are books, magazines, and useful websites that can change your life. Go after them!

Standing up for yourself is hard for many people who are hard of hearing. They do not want to ask the waiter to repeat what the specials of the day are, or ask their boss to stop covering his mouth when he talks. "I just do not want to be a nuisance," is a phrase that many people have said over the years.

The truth of the matter is that most people do not consider it a nuisance for people with hearing loss to offer suggestions for improving communication. Most people I have encountered would like to be told straight on what they can do better or differently. This is preferable to trying to guess, or being totally in the dark that you are not communicating effectively with a friend, family member or co-worker.

I must always follow up talking about "standing up for yourself" with some words of caution. If you are belligerent, condescending or abusive when you speak to people, they will focus on your strong emotions, not on your smart advice. While it is true that it is right and just for people to make small changes that ultimately make life better for you, how you say something is often more important than what you say.

I also caution people with hearing loss to not become exasperated when you have to gently and repeatedly recommend to the people around you what they need to do to help you. People forget easily, and will never understand the complexities of your hearing. This does not mean they do not care. It is actually a good thing that people forget about your hearing loss from time to time. They see the person in front of them first, and not the hearing loss.

### What happens when you decide to do what needs to be done?

Rocky Stone, the founder of Self Help for Hard of Hearing People (SHHH), told me one day that people will fight vigorously, tirelessly and with all their strength for life itself, but are not as likely to do that for their quality of life. This chapter, "Help for Your Hearing Loss," has really been about deciding to improve your quality of life. Managing one's own hearing loss can be discouraging and tiring.

You may often feel like saying, "This is not worth the bother anymore," which is understandable.

I encourage you to talk about your frustrations and fatigue with others who understand. Go to our SHHH website (*www. hearingloss.org*) and talk to people on a forum, or find a local group of people who know exactly what it is you are dealing with. You would be surprised how many thousands of people feel the same way you do.

What happens when you decide to seek help? First of all, you do not feel as powerless to do something about your hearing loss. You feel you are taking charge of it, even though you cannot fix it. Whether you know it or not, you also encourage others to deal with other types of problems they are having. You touch other lives, whether you ever realize it or not.

Helen Keller said her blindness cut her off from things, but her loss of hearing cut her off from people. By owning your hearing loss, by managing it, you refuse to be cut off from the people around you. That not only makes you better, but makes them better as well. Your life still has meaning, and you can make a difference, with or without "normal" hearing. Zachary Scott said, "As you grow older, you'll find that the only things you regret are the things you didn't do."

# Case Study of Bilateral Cochlear Implants

*by Jon K. Shallop, Ph.D. and Colin L.W. Driscoll, M.D.*

## Bilateral Cochlear Implants: Objective Assessment of Device Function and Variable Mode Programming in a case of Severe Facial Nerve Stimulation

Jon K. Shallop, Ph.D. and
Colin L.W. Driscoll, M.D.

Mayo Clinic, Department of Otorhinolaryngology
200 First Street SW  Ei2-140  Rochester, MN 55905

 MAYO CLINIC

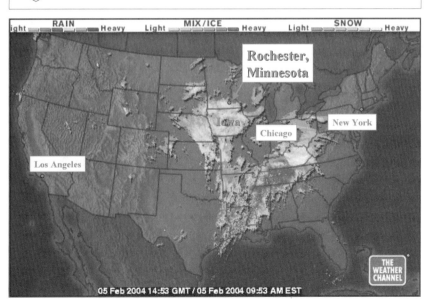

> Aug '96 Nucleus CI22M implanted Right
> Sept '96 Initial programming in BP+1 caused facial stimulation in middle electrodes 12-18
> Word and sentence scores decreased over next 5 years
> Jan 01 Nucleus CI24M implanted Left

> Jan '03 Patient comes to Mayo clinic requesting re-programming of CI22M Right
> MAP 94 – BP+1 mode had 8 active channels using electrodes 2,3,4,6 and 17,18 19,20.
> Word and sentence recognition was poor
> Patient experienced non-auditory sensations when the program was active

Patient presents to us with 2 major problems.
- 1. She is unable to use her N22 implant effectively.
- 2. Her N22 implant has migrated from its original position because the device was not secured by the surgeon with sutures. The implant is now touching the microphone and is causing RF interference.

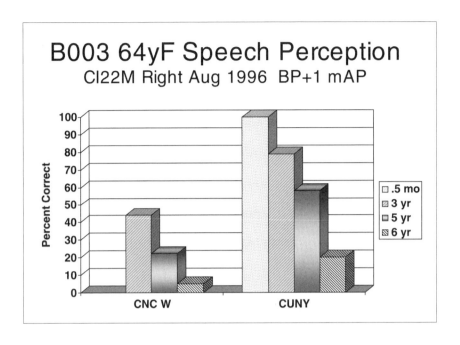

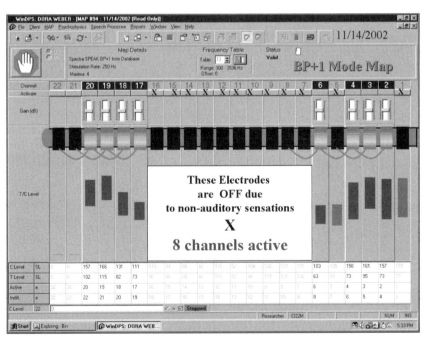

**Jan '03 Evaluation and Programming**

➢ **Crystal Integrity Test of both implants**

➢ **Verification of non-auditory stimulation**

➢ **Re-programming in variable modes**

➢ **Surgical revision of implant positioning**

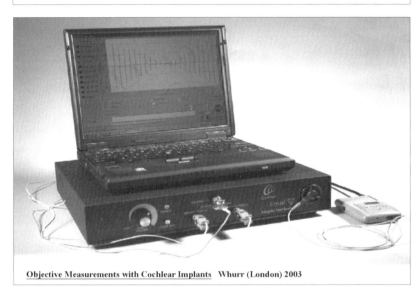

**Objective Measurements with Cochlear Implants** Whurr (London) 2003

*Cochlear Implants-Objective Measures*,
Edited by Helen Cullington. Whurr (London) 2003
Chapter 4, Shallop et al.

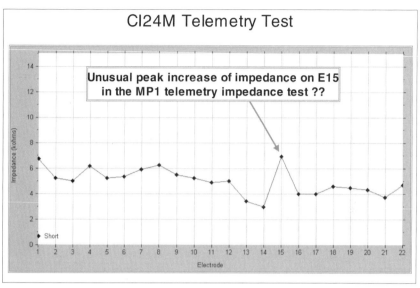

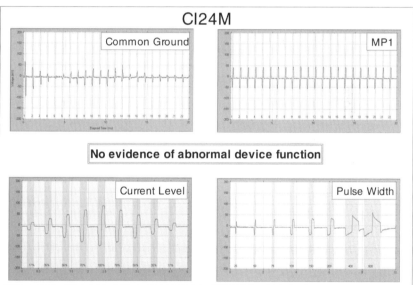

# Crystal Integrity Test of both implants
**N24 – overall normal except for increased impedance on electrode 15.**

# Crystal Integrity Test of both implants
N22 – overall normal except for phase reversal patterns and facial stimulation effects.

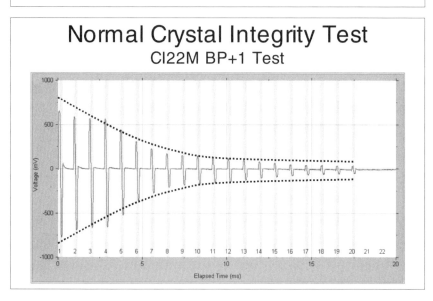

## Normal Crystal Integrity Test
### CI22M BP+1 Test

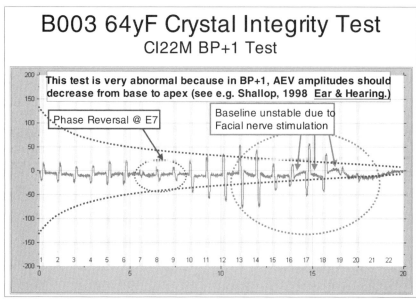

## B003 64yF Crystal Integrity Test
### CI22M BP+1 Test

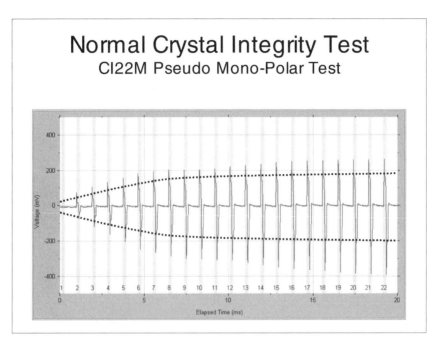

# Normal Crystal Integrity Test
## Cl22M Pseudo Mono-Polar Test

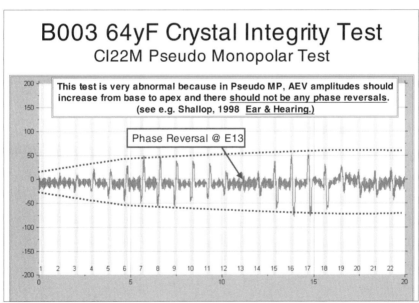

# B003 64yF Crystal Integrity Test
## Cl22M Pseudo Monopolar Test

This test is very abnormal because in Pseudo MP, AEV amplitudes should increase from base to apex and there should not be any phase reversals. (see e.g. Shallop, 1998 Ear & Hearing.)

Phase Reversal @ E13

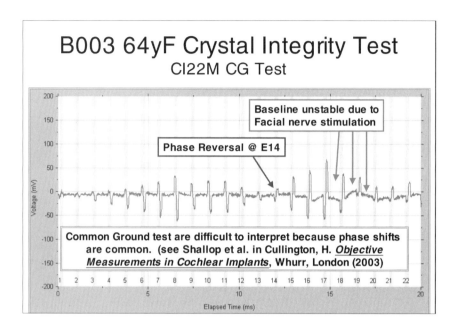

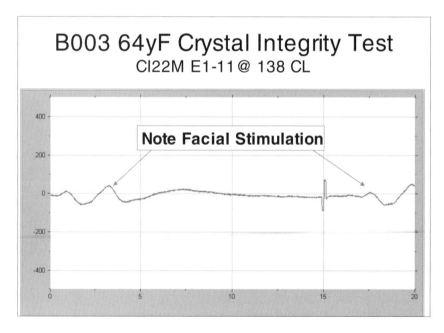

# Facial Nerve Stimulation

The American Journal of Otology
18:336-341 © 1997, The American Journal of Otology, Inc.

## Facial Nerve Stimulation After Nucleus 22-Channel Cochlear Implantation

*David C. Kelsall, †Jon K. Shallop, *Thomas G. Brammeier, and ‡Erin C. Prenger

*Denver Ear Associates, Denver; †Denver Ear Institute, Englewood;
and ‡Swedish Medical Center, Englewood; Colorado, U.S.A.

**Objective:** To review the clinical features, radiographic findings, and programming strategies used in our population of patients who developed facial nerve stimulation after cochlear implantation.
**Study Design and Setting:** Patients referred to our nonprofit, outpatient facility were studied prospectively.
**Patients:** The study consisted of 14 patients with facial nerve stimulation after placement of the Nucleus 22-channel cochlear implant.
**Interventions:** Records were reviewed retrospectively, and patients were studied with three-dimensional computed tomographic scanning techniques. Electrical testing was performed, and various cochlear implant programming strategies were evaluated.
**Main Outcome Measures:** Important clinical features were reviewed. The radiographic and anatomical relationships of the facial nerve to the cochlea were evaluated, and the pro-
gramming strategies used to effectively control facial nerve stimulation were reviewed.
**Results:** Prevalence of facial nerve stimulation in our population was 7%. The most common cause was otosclerosis. Anatomical data confirmed the close proximity of the basal turn of the cochlea and the labyrinthine segment of the facial nerve. There was a high correlation between the electrodes causing symptoms and those found radiographically to be closest to the labyrinthine segment of the facial nerve. We were able to control facial nerve stimulation in all patients through programming mode changes.
**Conclusions:** Otosclerosis appears to be a risk factor for developing facial nerve stimulation after cochlear implantation, and the site of stimulation appears to be the labyrinthine segment of the facial nerve. Familiarity with more elaborate programming techniques is critical to managing patients with this complication. **Key Words:** Cochlear implantation—Facial nerve stimulation. *Am J Otol* **18:**336–341, 1997.

The American Journal of Otology
18:336-341 © 1997, The American Journal of Otology, Inc.

### Anatomical study

In the five temporal bones dissected, electrodes 12–16 (average 14.8) were in the closest proximity to the labyrinthine portion of the facial nerve. The average bone thickness measurements for the four sites studied are presented in Table 2. The thinnest bone measured was between the labyrinthine segment of the facial nerve 1.0 mm from the geniculate ganglion and the basal turn of the cochlea with an average thickness of 0.52 mm (range 0.50–0.56).

### Radiographic study

Conventional temporal bone CT scans showed only two patients with radiographic abnormalities of the inner ear.

**TABLE 2.** *Thickness of bone separating facial canal and basal turn of cochlea*

| Facial nerve segment | Thickness (mm) | Range (mm) |
|---|---|---|
| Petrosal | 0.87 | 0.73–1.00 |
| Proximal labyrinthine | 0.75 | 0.67–0.83 |
| Midlabyrinthine | 0.52 | 0.50–0.56 |
| Distal labyrinthine | 0.67 | 0.56–0.83 |

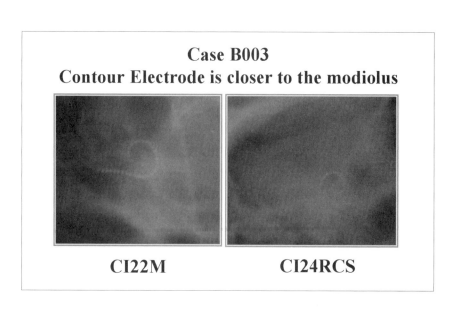

**Case B003**
**Contour Electrode is closer to the modiolus**

CI22M          CI24RCS

## Initial intervetions:

- 1. N22 is re-positioned in a revision surgery to a more typical position and secured.

- 2. She is re-programmed in variable mode to enable better tonotopic pitch perception.

# Note how the receiver stimulator had moved inferior in close proximity to the pinna.

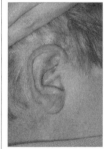   

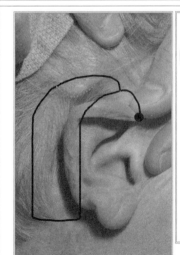 

**3G was over the bottom tip of the N22 implant.**

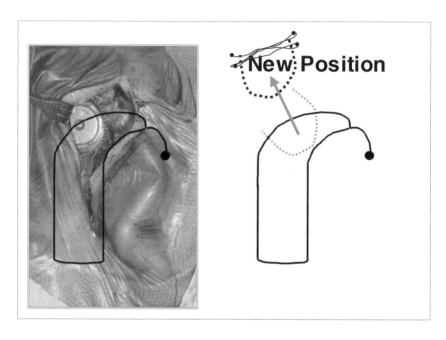

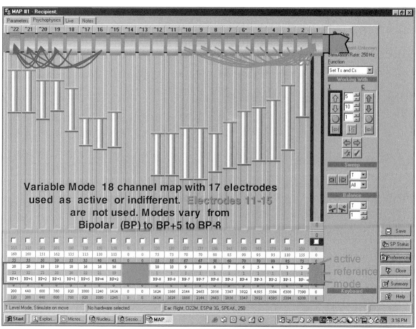

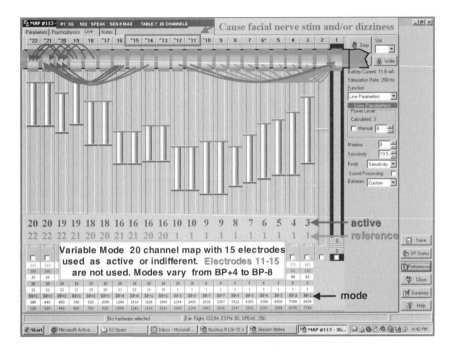

# Case B003

- **Patient is now using both cochlear implants**
- **All facial stimulation and pain is resolved. No RF interference.**
- **"I especially enjoy music with both"**
- **"I can detect direction of voices'**
- **"My Right implant (CI22M) sounds squeaky by itself, but together the quality of sound is very natural"**

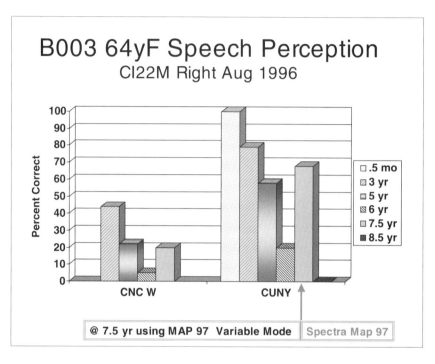

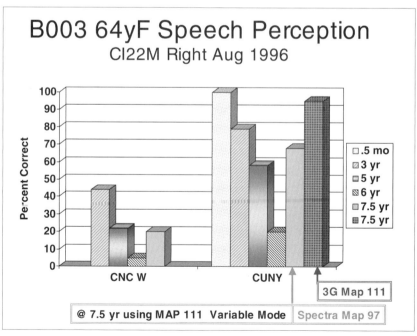

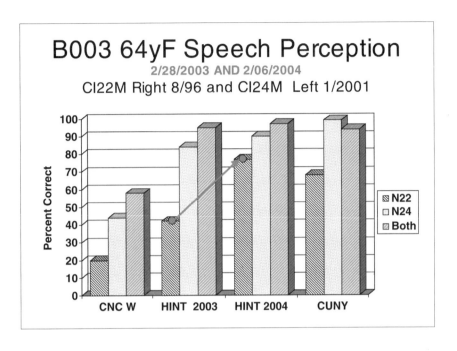

# Recommended Reading

*Sounds from Silence: The Bionic Ear Story*
by Professor Graeme Clark
Allen and Unwin

*Journey Out of Silence*
by Dora Tingelstad Weber
Beaver's Pond Press

*The Parent's Guide to Cochlear Implants*
by Patricia M. Chute and Mary Nevins
Galludet University Press

*Living with Hearing Loss*
by Marcia Dugan
Galludet University Press

*Do You Hear Me? Laughs for the Hard of Hearing by the Hard of Hearing*
by Maxwell Schneider
Thinking Publications

*Listen with the Heart*
by Michael A. Harvey, Ph.D.
Dawn Sign Press

*Our Forgotten Children: Hard of Hearing Pupils in the Schools*
edited by Julia M. Davis, Ph.D
SHHH Publications

*A Quiet World: Living with Hearing Loss*
by David G. Myers
Yale University Press

# For Information on Hearing Loss and Cochlear Implants

Mayo Clinic and College of Medicine
Cochlear Implant Facility
200 First Street
Rochester, Minnesota 55905

Association of Late Deafened Adults
(ALDA)
1131 Lake Street #204
Oak Park, Illinois 60301
Voice/Fax 877-907-1738
TTY 708-358-0135

Alexander Graham Bell Association
for the Deaf and Hard of Hearing
(AG Bell)
3417 Volta Place NW
Washington, D.C. 20007
866-337-5220 (toll free)
(202)-337-5220
TTY (202)337-5221
Fax (202)337-5221

Colorado Neurological Institute
Center for Hearing (CNI)
701 E. Hampden Ave., Suite 330
Englewood, Colorado 80113
Voice 303-806-7416
Voice 303-788-4010
Fax 788-788-5469
JStucky@theCNI.org
www.theCNI.org/hearing

Self Help for Hard of Hearing People
(SHHH)
7910 Woodmont Ave., Suite 1200
Bethesda, Maryland 20814
Voice 301-657-2248
TTY 301-657-2249
Fax 301-913-9413
www.hearingloss.org
info@hearingloss.org

Cochlear Corporation
400 Inverness Parkway
Suite 400
Englewood,Colorado 80112
Telephone: 1-303-790-9010

Advanced Bionics Corporation
12740 San Fernando Road
Sylmar, California 91342
Telephone: 1-661-362-1400

Med-El Corporation (North America)
2222 East Highway 54
Beta Building, Suite 180
Durham, North Carolina 27713
Telephone: 1-919-572-2222

# About the Author

In her first book, *Journey Out of Silence*, Dora Weber shared her life as a hearing person, the hard times which occurred as she gradually lost her hearing, and the joy she experienced when her hearing was restored with her Nucleus 22 cochlear implant. In an effort to encourage others to "never give up," Dora wrote this book to relate her trials when her hearing began to fade away and to tell of her triumph when she regained it.

Dora has participated in several extensive research studies. She is the co-founder of *Cochlear Implant News and Views,* the Mayo Cochlear Implant newsletter, and serves as a volunteer advocate for Cochlear Americas. In addition, she frequently shares her story with church, medical and civic organizations.

Dora and her husband, Myron, have been married for 43 years and are the parents of four sons. They have six grandchildren: Jeffery, Justin, Jacob, Chelsea, Brandon, and Ashley.

Myron and Dora live in Spring Lake Park, Minnesota. They are members of Prince of Peace Lutheran Church.